It's On Me

It's On Me

ACCEPT HARD TRUTHS, DISCOVER YOUR SELF,
AND CHANGE YOUR LIFE.

Sara Kuburic

THE DIAL PRESS

NEW YORK

Published in the United States by The Dial Press, an imprint of Random House, a division of Penguin Random House LLC, New York.

THE DIAL PRESS is a registered trademark and the colophon is a trademark of Penguin Random House LLC.

LIBRARY OF CONGRESS CATALOGING-IN-PUBLICATION DATA
Names: Kuburic, Sara, author.
Title: It's on me / Sara Kuburic.
Other titles: It is on me
Description: First edition. | New York: The Dial Press, [2023]
Identifiers: LCCN 2023018741 (print) | LCCN 2023018742 (ebook) |
ISBN 9780593449264 (hardcover) | ISBN 9780593449288 (ebook)
Subjects: LCSH: Self-perception. | Introspection. | Self-realization. |
Self-actualization (Psychology)
Classification: LCC BF697.5.S43 K83 2023 (print) | LCC BF697.5.S43 (ebook) |
DDC 158.1—dc23/eng/20230606
LC record available at https://lccn.loc.gov/2023018741
LC ebook record available at https://lccn.loc.gov/2023018742

International ISBN 978-0-593-73064-5

Printed in the United States of America on acid-free paper

randomhousebooks.com

9 8 7 6 5 4 3 2 1

First Edition

Book design by Caroline Cunningham

Author's Note

The life experiences we each have and share are intimate and sacred; they belong to us and can never be fully grasped by others—the best a reader can do is hear them, interpret them, and learn from them. They are on loan, with the original pulse stored within those who lived them. This is why I am utterly grateful for all who were willing to share their stories with me, who were willing to offer me the most precious glimpses into their existence.

This book is rooted in my theoretical and clinical expertise, but it is inspired by my own experiences and conversations that I've had with people I know and work with. Every client, friend, and research participant has been given a pseudonym and has had their identifying characteristics changed. The conversations I recall have been altered in an effort to protect privacy and honor confidentiality. In addition, my biographical details are at times slightly tweaked as a way to preserve my own sense of privacy and safety, while still maintaining the integrity of my own lived experience.

Lastly, philosophy is a tricky beast and although I've done my best to distill some complex ideas, I encourage you to do your own reading and reach your own truth.

To All Who Feel Lost

Contents

PART III: The Self You Live

PART IV: The Self You Are

It's On Me

I Don't Know Who I Am

"**A**re you happy?"

The question catches me off-guard, as does my instinct to respond: *No, not at all. I am simply enduring the fact that I am alive.*

I am stunned.

I'm twenty-four years old, visiting L.A. for the weekend and having drinks with a close friend from college, someone I haven't seen much since graduation. The conversation had been light—reminiscing about our carefree days at school, cringing and laughing at the memories. But then he'd leveled me with the seemingly innocuous question:

"Are you happy?"

While I don't say it out loud, this is the first time I've *allowed* myself to acknowledge the fact that I am deeply unhappy. *Why now?* At this intersection of truth and raw emotion—the moment I will, years later, recognize in my clients when they realize, suddenly and irrepressibly, that an aspect of their life no longer feels honest to them—tears begin to roll down my face. My friend stares at me, bewildered.

I sit there, feeling ambushed and betrayed by my body. My chest starts to heave as my lungs fight to find air between sobs. I don't say anything; instead, I plummet into disjointed and booming thoughts.

I am deeply, profoundly unhappy.

I don't know who I am anymore—and I don't remember the last time I did.

I feel broken—but I don't remember breaking.

I tell my friend I need to use the bathroom. Unsteadily, I find my way to the sink and grasp its edges to anchor myself. A scream is building inside of me, but I don't let it out. I splash water on my face and neck, hoping the cold will snap me back into a reality that hurts a little less.

When I finally look in the mirror, I am met with hollow, unfamiliar eyes. They're empty. *Is anyone even in there?* I lift my arm to wipe my face, and the stranger mirrors me. The woman touching my cheeks is me, but *she* doesn't feel like *me*. I feel utterly disconnected from the person staring back. *Is this who everyone else sees?*

I am dizzy, inexplicably overwhelmed.

Then, it finally dawns on me: *I HATE the woman in the mirror.* I am confused, frustrated, and constantly hurt by her.

Fuck her! I suffer as she just watches me live a life that I am not even sure is worth living.

So, no . . .

"I am not happy," I finally say out loud, in an empty bathroom, to no one in particular.

———————

The next morning, I have a plane to catch—my sister and I have been in Los Angeles for a "girls' trip" and are heading back home to Vancouver. I was able to pull myself together at the bar the night before, but now the dread of going back to my "real" life is palpable. As I pack my bag, I feel heavier with each piece of clothing I put in my suitcase. I begin to wonder about all the people, things, and roles I've "placed" into my life that weren't meant for me. Then I quickly chastise myself, feeling ungrateful, even ashamed of my discontent. By the age of nine, I had survived the Bosnia and Kosovo Wars, and the fact that I am alive, healthy, and living in Canada is an enormous and wonderful privilege. I have food, shelter, and fresh ocean air. *Things are good!*

But of course, this forced positivity only makes me feel shittier.

The truth is, I am finding it hard to be grateful these days. I live in a dark, crappy one-bedroom basement apartment that my husband and I can barely afford. The beat-up van I drive makes an embarrassing amount of noise every time I push the brake. I got married the summer before grad school, at the tender age of twenty-two, and in the conservative, Christian community in which I grew up, no one flinched as I made such a huge commitment before my frontal cortex had even fully developed. *Why didn't anyone stop me?* I wonder. Now I come home to a husband I don't love. Luckily, I am gone most days attending classes and studying for my master's program in counseling psychology—but even my refuge is exhausting and competitive. With each assignment, my flaws and past traumas have become glaringly obvious. In addition to my academic requirements, I am asked to learn about and navigate other people's emotional pain in therapy sessions, while simultaneously trying to manage my own. I spend a lot of my time daydreaming about having a very different life—fantasizing about the endless could-have-beens—as a way to cope with my reality. Lately I've noticed that my senses have dulled, making me feel detached, almost, from my own existence.

I feel pressured to be someone I am not and to live a life that I don't want. People assume my life is fun, sweet, idyllic even, and it's become my job to keep up the pretenses—the perfect marriage, the slim figure, the academic accomplishments. Yet, as hard as I try, I feel like I'm failing—myself and the people around me.

I am drowning.

I am asked to be many things: wife, student, therapist, friend, daughter, and sibling. But no one is asking me to be my Self, to show up as who I really am—and it wouldn't matter if they did, because even I don't know who that really is. I have no space to unravel my thoughts or decipher my feelings, although maybe that's just an excuse, because I have the sneaking suspicion that if I did, I would come undone. I feel trapped, frightened that all my decisions—big and small—have set a sentence, without parole, for a life I don't want. Deep down, I know that the only way to escape is to shatter my life as I know it.

But what if, in the process, *I* shatter instead? What if I break before I can break free?

In the cab on my way to the airport, I'm sweating profusely, digging my nails into my palms to prevent myself from vomiting. *Nothing* about my body feels right. I can't even hold a simple conversation with my sister; my thoughts are racing. By the time we arrive, my senses are flooded. The crowds, the mixed smells of fast food and coffee, and the heaviness of supporting my body as I stand in line to board the plane—it's all just *too much*.

As the discomfort intensifies, I try even harder to ignore it. (What is it about humans that we would rather endure suffering than face our truth?) I deny my reality pretty successfully until we are seated on the plane and the seatbelt sign illuminates for takeoff. As I click in, my vision becomes blurry, my breath short, and my skin feels too tight. I am desperate to claw my way out—out of this seat, out of my body, out of my life. The tin-can walls of the plane are closing in and the air feels thicker, stale. Sweat drips down my neck and chest. I unbuckle and stand up, pushing my way toward the front of the plane. Confused passengers stare as the flight attendant repeatedly asks me to sit down.

"I need to get off. I need to get off now!" I scream. Something is happening. *Nothing* is going to stop me.

I don't even remember leaving the plane, but suddenly I am

standing at an empty airport gate looking at my sister with sheer panic.

My legs tingle. Then my upper body seizes. My arms fold into themselves, curling my hands toward my chest as my wrists twist and my fingers contort into claws. *I am trapped in my body*. My sister runs to look for medical assistance. *Holy hell*. I am terrified as I watch her disappear into the distance. She comes back minutes (but it feels like *hours*) later, just in time to watch me lose my ability to speak. I can no longer move my jaw or lips, and words are coming out as groans.

Then, as suddenly as the symptoms hit, my mind clears. I am focused.

It's funny how unrestricted we become when we believe we're facing death. In this moment, I realize that I am willing to do anything to protect myself, because *nothing* is worth this feeling. *What if I die before I even have a chance to truly exist?* I wonder.

Looking at myself head-on and changing my life no longer feels like a suggestion; it is a necessity. I am willing to adjust, burn, toss, abandon, or shatter anything. One thought rings loudest: *I will be there for myself. I will no longer be a passive observer in my own damn life.*

Several minutes later, the paramedics arrive. I am not dying; I've had my first panic attack. They give me a pill and ask me to breathe. They are calm, and I am confused by their nonchalance—*I've just stared death in the face!* But indeed, a couple of minutes later, my speech comes back, my arms unfold, and I can stand.

Today, I understand that my panic attack occurred in response to my *recognition* of my profound loss—the fact that I was engulfed in a life that wasn't right for me and that I was struggling to *be* my Self. This event itself didn't change my life, but it forced me to realize that nothing in my life would change until *I* made adjustments. Part of finally taking responsibility for my life meant recognizing when I was being the problem. It meant looking inward and accepting that, at the end of the day, it was on me to accept the fact that my choices had created my realities, and to take the necessary steps to change things.

So, in the months after that airport panic attack, I became intentional about creating space for the version of my Self I *wanted* to be—to grow and evolve. Instead of controlling or limiting who I was (or allowing others to do so), I learned to just let my Self *be*. And in this way of existing, I began to feel more known, seen, and understood than I ever had before— not by others but by myself. I learned who I was, and finally, I learned to live as my Self.

Concretely, I ended my marriage. I took a sabbatical from my studies. I stopped seeing clients for a period. I withdrew from friends who I felt didn't have my best interests at heart. I set boundaries and consequently—and dramatically—lost or transformed many of the relationships that were contributing to my anxiety or existential dread. I began to listen to my body *very* carefully. I acknowledged the cage of expectations I had been living in. I packed my suitcase, confirmed the eight hundred dollars in my checking account, asked a friend if I could sleep on their couch, and got on a flight to the town in Serbia I grew up in (with no idea what I would do there or when I would come back). I wrote in my journal. I let myself cry. I began to face the trauma of my war-ridden past. I didn't have sex again until I truly wanted to. I ate and moved in a way that honored my body. I grieved the self-relationship I never had. I listened to and questioned what I had to say. I rested. I learned to make all of this a practice, an ongoing and repeated effort that shaped my life. And, most important, I took *responsibility* for my own existence.

When I returned to school, I completed my master's in counseling psychology and went on to finish a doctoral program in psychotherapy science. I became an existential therapist, helping clients with identity, relationships, trauma, and, well, existential issues (more on what those are, exactly, later). I began to work with individuals who felt empty, disconnected, frustrated, or simply unhappy about the life they were living or the self they were being.

In my sessions, I began to see one common thread:

Self-loss.

Self-loss is what I believe to be at the core of so much of our human suffering. Although most of us can intuitively grasp what the phrase "self-loss" means, it's likely that we've never heard of it or had it explained. *Self-loss is our failed responsibility to BE our Self.* It's not a concept that you will stumble upon in the *DSM-5* or in most therapy rooms, but it is an inherently human experience that's been expressed in novels, art, music, and in most of our lives.

Once I had lived it, it was easy to recognize self-loss in others, and it was fascinating to watch my own experience echo in the narratives I would hear from my clients and research participants over the years. And so, this is why I wrote this book: to help you explore the concept of self-loss, so that you can answer for yourself what are arguably the two most daunting questions:

Who am I?
Why am I here?

I won't, or rather I *can't,* give you the answers. Instead, I will show you how to *live inside these questions.* Life is messy and complicated; we need to let go of the idea that being human is easy and straightforward. Let's stop pretending there are definitive answers to all of life's questions or that we are all headed to a single destination of happiness or success. That's not possible, that place doesn't exist. But you will see that a life in which you constantly ask questions—and take responsibility for living your own personal and individual answers—is an existence that is wildly liberating and profoundly meaningful.

Many of us experience pain from resisting who we are and what we want—by not being open to the absurdity of existence, and to the unknown ways in which life unfolds. My panic attack, albeit excruciating, was the distinct moment that placed me on the profound and exhilarating path toward embodying who I truly am. Today, that memory is colored in gratitude;* without it, I could still be wandering, wondering

---

* This is not to imply that we should always be "grateful" for painful life experiences.

who I am and why I am even here. Or worse yet, I would still be *simply, and perpetually, enduring the fact that I am alive.*

I finally feel *free*—free to express myself; to taste the wine I drink and to smell the ocean outside my window. People in my life are genuine and supportive. My "roles" align with who I am—they are lived from a place of resonance rather than obligation. I make choices that honor me, as I embrace the ongoing task of *being* my Self. When I look in a mirror, I recognize the person staring back at me, and I am proud of her.

So, please join me on this dynamic, beautiful, worthwhile journey of existence—to consistently, at every moment, *choose* who you are and to say *yes* to the people, places, and things that give *you* meaning. To say *yes* to facing, accepting, and fully owning your one beautiful life, and, even more important, your Self.

PART I

The Self

To dare is to lose one's footing momentarily. Not to dare is to lose oneself.

—ATTRIBUTED TO SØREN KIERKEGAARD

CHAPTER 1

What Is Self-Loss?

Here's a visualization I often do with my clients to give them a sense of what self-loss feels like:

Imagine you're alone, sitting in a worn leather armchair in the middle of a room. In front of you is a chipped coffee table straining to support the weight of the numerous dusty books that you intended to read but never found time for. You have a cup of coffee that has grown cold, the milk curdled on the surface. On the side table next to you is a vintage green lamp, merely ornamental ever since the room has been set ablaze.

The flames are creeping up the walls, peeling the wallpaper and sending parachutes of ash in midair. The flares slowly inch toward you; little sparks burning holes in the rug at your feet. You can barely see through the haze; your lungs fill with smoke, your eyes water. Yet you continue to sit there—paying bills, checking your email, making work deadlines, sending long, upset text messages, or posting inspirational quotes on Instagram—ignoring your impending death. You hear faint instinctual inner screams. A voice deep inside is urging you to MOVE.

But instead, you convince yourself that "this is fine"; that you are fine, in control, even. That the way you have chosen to live will not hurt you. Your life is threatened, but for some reason or another you don't see it; you ignore it, or perhaps you're waiting for someone else to save you. You are too "busy" to save yourself. Or, maybe you notice the flames, but you are preoccupied with debating who set the fire in the first place—you'd rather figure out who to blame than find a way to live. Regardless of the specifics, you don't choose to extinguish the fire, which ultimately means you are choosing to get burned.

I ask my clients to sit with, explore, and make meaning of this metaphor. When they have constructed their own interpretation, I share my intent:

We are alone in the room because that's a given—no one will ever truly know what it's like to be us. The old, worn armchair represents the comfort we feel from the habits and patterns we've developed. It's placed in the center of the room because we are often—for better or for worse—the focal point of our own lives. Our strained relationships (the table) are burdened by our lack of self-growth and healing (the unopened books). The cold coffee represents time passing, and complacency settling in. The lamp repre-

sents our dimming awareness, its light overpowered by the flames (our denial) creeping up the walls.

The wallpaper represents our boundaries. Over time, it begins to peel off and compromise the integrity of the room, of who we are. The rug, our foundation—beliefs, morals, values—is set ablaze and we struggle to find our footing. The blurred vision is the detrimental stories we tell ourselves, and the smoke filling our lungs is all the things we consume that we believe will make us "whole," but don't. We successfully ignore signs of danger and the call to responsibility. We surrender our freedom and risk our lives to enjoy the warmth of the familiar—our so-called obligations and day-to-day mundanities. We may not know why we find ourselves in a burning room or who is to blame, but ultimately the only thing that matters is what we do about it.

It can be hard to wrap our heads around the idea of facing such a clear threat and continuing to live as if it's of no consequence. It's difficult to imagine that someone on the verge of losing something as significant as their Self* can ignore the warning signs. This loss—this impending danger that I am talking about—is not physical, it is existential.

* Throughout the book you will notice that sometimes I capitalize the S in "Self" and sometimes I do not. Whenever it is capitalized, I am referring to our authentic being. Whenever I use "self" or "yourself" instead of "your Self," I am referring to the inauthentic or lost version of who we are. For consistency's sake (and because it's possible to experience self-loss without ever having known your true Self), "self-loss" is always lowercase.

And it's the danger that most of us face as a consequence of the way we choose to live our everyday lives.

Let's spend a day in the life of a girl named Alex. When her alarm goes off in the morning, the first thing she does is grab her phone. It will only take a couple of seconds before her finger taps on the first app. As her eyes adjust to the brightness, she will squint away the blur of her screen and check her DMs, silently calculating when to respond or like a picture without looking too eager. She will mindlessly scroll for a couple of minutes, or ten, or twenty-five, consciously or subconsciously taking note of other people's lives, body shapes, or success, adding new insecurities, comparisons, or expectations to the back of her mind. Eventually she will hurry around her apartment to get ready (for the gaze of others), and if there is enough time to do one thing for herself that morning—it's going to be *coffee*. Always. Alex will chug it as she hops on her first online meeting or rushes out the door to catch the train, completely forgetting to eat breakfast, drink water . . . or take a deep breath.

At work, she puts on a faint smile while dealing with people who are unpleasant, unkind, or just bad at their jobs. She lives by her online calendar, which tells her who to talk to and when, and which tasks she needs to tackle. She often checks her emails during long calls, paying very little attention to either. If she is feeling annoyed, she'll send a snarky text to a colleague on the same video call—waiting to see if they crack a smile. At lunch, she will get a caffeine refill and eat some food, while barely taking a moment to notice its taste. She will take a picture of her outfit or the view from her desk— commenting on the weather, her workload, or making a self-deprecating joke. Every two or three minutes, Alex will check to see who's viewed her story and look at it herself—her pictures tend to paint her life better than she knows how to live it, and looking at them helps her feel like she's living much more than she actually is.

After work, she might hop on her Peloton, not because she cares about her health but because she hates her body. Afterward, she will meet up with her friends or watch Netflix on the couch in an effort to distract herself from feeling drained, upset, bored, or unfulfilled, while spending the majority of the time glancing at her phone, wondering if that person she's seeing is going to text her back. Eventually she crawls into bed and looks at her screen until her eyelids get heavy.

Alex has become accustomed to (some might even say comfortable with) living in the burning room.

And with every passing day, she sinks deeper into self-loss.

Does any of this feel familiar?

The term "self-loss" almost sounds like we can misplace our essence like a set of car keys or our phone charger. And although arguably a tempting explanation, it would be inaccurate to compare self-loss to losing some*thing* or some*one* else. Simply put: **Self-loss is being estranged from and lacking congruence, resonance, and alliance with who we truly are.** It's the feeling of being inconsistent and inauthentic—of having our actions, feelings, and decisions cease to represent how we understand and experience ourselves as "truly" being.

The regrettable reality is that too many of us go on with life unfazed by the fact that *we do not know who we are*. As an existential therapist, I have come to understand that the human sense of Self is the staple of well-being, relationships, and fulfillment. Self-loss, on the other hand, is often why we fail to communicate and set boundaries, why we hold on to beliefs that no longer serve us, why we struggle in relationships, why we are overwhelmed or scared to make decisions, why self-love is so *goddamn* difficult, and finally, why so many of us fail to find meaning and purpose in our lives.

If you are reading this, chances are that you spend much of your time feeling like the walking dead, not fully conscious, vibrant, or free. This state of existence is so common that, at this point, I would be as bold as to say that self-loss has become part of the human condition. It is not pathological, it is not a diagnosis (although it can be comorbid with other mental health struggles). It is something many of us face and it is *the* obstacle that stands in the way of authenticity, fulfillment, and meaningful connection with others.

The crux of self-loss is that it doesn't allow us to exist—not truly. Not in a way we find fulfilling or, perhaps, even worth all the effort.

More often than not, our self-loss is a result of the way we live our seemingly routine and, at times, mundane lives. It manifests through our daily choices and actions, ultimately—and often subtly—leading us to the point where we no longer recognize, or connect with, our Self. This loss feels like detachment, or estrangement from our feelings, body, thoughts, beliefs, relationships, meaning, freedom, values. The disconnect makes it impossible to act with alignment and consistency (because what would you even be aligning with?). And, after a while, this dissonance creates an unspoken and haunting feeling of emptiness, fragmentation, or incongruence that we ignore and deny for as long as we can bear it.

Søren Kierkegaard, a Danish philosopher, once said that self-loss "causes little stir in the world; for in the world a self is what one least asks after, and the thing it is most dangerous of all to show signs of having. The biggest danger, that of losing oneself, can pass off in the world as quietly as if it were nothing; every loss, an arm, a leg, five dollars, a wife, etc. is bound to be unnoticed."

The paradox of this loss is that although it often goes unnoticed, it still involves our will. Meaning, it ultimately happens because *we allow it to*. We do not lose our Self without our permission or participation. *We may not choose to be in a burning room, but our inaction, our neglect to extinguish the flames, becomes a decision.* It may be our lack of awareness, a particularly unhealthy environment or relationship, or an old wound that drives the estrangement in the first place. But more often than not, the self-loss—the complete disconnect from who we are—is ultimately accomplished through the process of self-deception. The threat is so big that the only way we can cope with it—besides actually doing something about it—is to lie to ourselves and deny that we feel empty, unfulfilled, and confused. Life has become a patchwork consisting of our misguided efforts to fill the void with relationships, jobs, possessions, or even, sometimes, kids. Anything that can help us pretend for just a little longer that there is nothing wrong. We continually ignore our past, our shadows, our wounds, and then wonder why we find ourselves making decisions that don't serve us.

Our propensity to self-deceive—to hide the truth from ourselves and see only what we want to see despite proof to the contrary—is not merely an individual quirk, but an approach to Self that is embedded within society as a whole. Our society has *normalized* being something other than our Self, and to be honest, most of us don't know that there is an alternative path. We've been taught to invent, pretend, morph, and edit who we are in an effort to achieve "belonging" or "recognition," as if such external gains will compensate for the emptiness within.

Some of us knew who we were and then we lost our way. Some of us never became our Self in the first place. We grew older, we aged, our roles and functions changed, but we never grasped our *essence* (the intrinsic quality that makes us who we are, a concept I will explore in further detail in the next chapter). We became many things—a professional, a partner, a mentor, a parent, a friend—but we never truly became our Self. We never took real responsibility for the precious, limited time we were given. Before we knew it, a deep sense of disorientation made it difficult for us to even know where to begin.

Self-loss, in its most basic function, restricts our ability to *be* our Self.

It is one of the most painful human experiences—an invisible suffering that colors *every* aspect of our lives. As a result of not knowing who we are, we:

Self-sabotage and hurt ourselves unintentionally.

Struggle to identify and verbalize what we need, think, or how we feel.

Find ourselves living a life that we don't want or don't find fulfilling.

Prioritize others over ourselves.

Stay in relationships that we are not meant to be in.

Get caught in cycles of reenacting unhealthy patterns.

Are unable to identify our purpose or direction in life.

Fail at setting and maintaining boundaries.

Are faced with a deep sense of unhappiness.

Grapple with our self-esteem.

Are constantly overwhelmed or disappointed by life.

Find it hard, ultimately, to truly connect with, accept, and trust who we are.

HOW DOES SELF-LOSS MANIFEST?

I didn't address my own self-loss for a long time, mostly because I didn't know I was lost. One of the reasons it's challenging to pinpoint self-loss—besides our willing or unwilling ignorance—is because, for so many of us, it's deeply intertwined with the experience of being human.

I experienced the manifestation of self-loss in every aspect of my life:

I suppressed my emotions until they overwhelmed me.

I misused and ignored the signals my body was sending, until it forced me to listen.

I had a bad habit of forcing relationships to work because I didn't know who I was without them.

I lived a large part of my life blindly accepting a belief system that guided my morality. The issue wasn't the worldview per se, the issue was my lack of agency and attunement to my own needs and desires.

*And finally, while I appeared to be one of those boring
and always-responsible human beings, I was recklessly
irresponsible with my own existence. I lived as if I had
time to waste and wouldn't feel the consequences of my
actions. I deceived myself into thinking that being* unfulfilled, sad, and confused *was the way I was meant to
live my life.*

I wish I could have recognized my loss sooner, but that would
have required knowing what to look for—and I didn't. So, let
me help you get a better grasp of how self-loss generally manifests in our lives, *holistically.* Let's look at five major categories:

1. Emotions

     Individuals who experience self-loss often struggle to
     self-regulate, self-soothe, or emotionally connect—they
     lack inner grounding. As a consequence, they begin to
     cope through mechanisms of avoidance, suppression, or
     escapism.

     Some coping mechanisms are more obvious—like get-
     ting drunk every night or binge-watching TV. Other cop-
     ing mechanisms are difficult to detect because at first
     glance they may seem like admirable behaviors. For in-
     stance, many people make themselves *busy* or seek ac-
     complishments (society's badges of honor). We are
     constantly impressed by such people, rather than con-
     cerned about them (which would sometimes be a more
     appropriate response). They go through life managing to
     drown their loss by numbing or detaching from their feel-
     ings, being too busy to feel the pain.

The emotional impact of self-loss is often found in the extremes.

Some individuals will get irritated by others who display a lot of emotions (or, more accurately, they will get triggered by them). They will pity others for their "lack of control" and pat themselves on the back for having so much restraint as to not feel anything. They will view their approach to life as superior, and offer no space for others to sit with their emotions around them. I used to be like this.

On the other hand, others may experience self-loss as constantly feeling overwhelmed by their feelings (not knowing what to do with them). They may allow their emotions to dictate their actions and expect others to help them manage them, while struggling to make sense of what their emotions mean or are trying to communicate. For example, new mothers have been known to smash objects in their homes or punch walls. The imposition and violation of the Self that can come from having a child can translate to overwhelming rage and self-harm. Yes, it can be a symptom of postpartum rage, but it can also be a consequence of dissolution of Self, in the endless demands suddenly present.

2. The Body

We cannot separate our body from who we are. In this light, it is not surprising that when we experience self-loss, it makes it harder to feel alignment and congruency—meaning, it becomes difficult to find agreement, harmony, and compatibility with sex, food, movement (exercise), and our Self. We often misunderstand our physical needs, wants, preferences, or experiences. We are more likely to use our body as a tool than a form of expression or extension of who we are.

Many of us expect too much from our bodies, while paying very little attention to them (a recipe for any unhealthy relationship). We over-exercise, don't regulate stress, say cruel things about certain body parts (our thighs, stomachs, necks), don't get sufficient sleep, hydrate with coffee rather than with water, ignore signals of unease or distress, have sex in a way we don't want to, suppress our tears, and use our body as bait or a trophy rather than a living, breathing, changing entity. This is all because most of us don't understand our body as part of our *core* Self.

3. Relationships

The relationship we have with our Self will be reflected in the types of relationships we have with others. People who experience self-loss are more likely to enter into and remain in 1) unhealthy relationships, 2) one-sided relationships, 3) unfulfilling relationships, or 4) all of the above. Why? Because self-loss is often accompanied by our inability or unwillingness to discern which relationships align with how we feel, what we need, and who we are. When we lack self-understanding, we are more likely to choose a partner or relationship as a response to our wounds, insecurities, or modeled behavior.

Self-loss often robs us of our sense of worth and leaves us trying to regain our value through external validation.

Many of us can relate to forcing relationships to work by convincing ourselves that what our partner wants is what *we* want, that the way they treat us is "normal," or—my personal favorite—that "no one is perfect" as a way to excuse repeatedly crappy behaviors. This mindset can lead to many unfulfilling or painful dynamics (*to say the least*), as well as further our self-loss by not giving us space or permission to be our Self. Many of us end up not knowing who we are outside of a relationship. If you've ever felt really stuck on someone, chances are it's because you weren't sure who you were without them.

4. Inner Consent

Self-loss can lead to lack of inner consent. "Inner consent" is a term in existential analysis, a fancy way of saying *agreement* or *permission* for the way we are choosing to use our human freedom and live our life. When we experience self-loss, we often don't participate with intention or discernment, and, as a result, we struggle to defend or accept not just our circumstances, consequences, or responsibilities, but who we are.

Inner consent is our willingness to say *yes* to life— saying *yes* to our thoughts, values, emotionality, who we are, what matters to us, our convictions, our personal uniqueness, our attitude, our purpose. It is the practice of tuning in and evaluating whether something aligns or is in harmony with who we understand our Self to be.

When you look in the mirror, can you stand behind (and endorse) the person staring back at you and the way you show up from moment to moment? Can you feel at peace with your actions, even if others don't like them? Are you living your truth? Are you inspired by the life you're leading?

Giving inner consent is a necessary, ongoing practice because our existence happens as an accumulation of instances. It's not enough to just give our consent to a few big, life-altering decisions or events. If we don't consent to life incrementally, it may be more difficult to consent to the life we are living as a whole. When we give our inner consent, life stops happening *to* us. Instead it becomes something *for* us, to shape as we'd like.

Inner consent is an *empowered* stance.

Sometimes, saying *yes* actually means saying *no*. Bear with me. Sometimes, in order to say *yes* to our values, beliefs, wants, thoughts, or feelings, we have to say *no* to certain invitations, people, jobs, relationships, opinions, and worldviews. Saying *yes* to life is saying *yes* to taking responsibility for how we exist; it's not about agreeing to do everything we are offered or asked to do.

Inner consent is felt rather than merely thought, it's a deep sense of resonance—a feeling of "rightness." It is an affirming experience that allows us to fully show up, stand our ground, and express our Self. It is a feeling of complete agreement with our actions and who we perceive our Self to be. There is no inner consent without a clear idea of who we are. And, without inner consent, there is no authenticity or fulfillment.

5. Meaning and Morality

Meaning is the *reason* we choose to live, while morality dictates the *way* we choose to live. Meaning and morality are the direction—or orientation—toward which we point our existence. Self-loss is not merely a result of action or inaction; sometimes it's a consequence of misdirection. The impact of self-loss manifests as ambiguous values, morals, or ethical conduct; even meaninglessness. We often find ourselves having a difficult time discerning what we believe in or why, or how to purposefully engage with the world around us.

Growing up, many of us were taught that meaning came from our contribution to the world. Although many of us do find this fulfilling, this message focuses solely on meaning as a consequence of our *output* or "usefulness." This narrative can make us forget that we (yes, you— exactly as you are in this moment) hold meaning. Period. We have meaning within our Self—we have the power to create meaning from the way we engage with and understand the world, not just from how we contribute to it. It's important to learn that we can find meaning in a conversation, in an art gallery, or simply in watching the waves crash against a rock.

As for morality, individuals who grew up with a set of rules (morals) by which they abided often feel lost once they distance themselves from, change, or question their belief system. Many of my clients have learned the virtue of obedience, but most did not—or were not allowed to—think for themselves. Lack of questioning and reflection can translate into blind obedience, which does not take into account inner consent, attunement, or alignment. Preset morals dictated their actions, providing them a sort of cheat sheet, and shaping them into who they are—and for some, who they are is lost.

IT GETS BETTER

No one ever intends to lose their Self, but at some point, their intention becomes irrelevant. Not irrelevant in terms of responsibility, but irrelevant in terms of the consequences. If someone sets your house on fire—regardless of whether it's by accident or on purpose—the reality remains that there is a fire to deal with. Later on in this book, we will explore who or what may have lit the flame that eroded your Self, but remember, the origin of the spark will *never* be as important as what you decide to do about the inferno. It's unrealistic for us to expect ourselves to be fully authentic and aligned at every moment in our lives, but we *cannot* stop trying. We have a *responsibility* to be our Self (and, let's not forget, to offer ourself grace as we keep trying).

We must stop normalizing the painful experiences of self-loss. Although it's common, this is not a condition worth settling for. If we lose our Self, we will be left with a life we are merely enduring, performing. We deserve more, and we can have more.

It's easy to pathologize any human experience that involves suffering, but let's not dismiss the role pain can play in our lives. I am not suggesting we should seek out pain, but rather that we can gain insight from it when it does happen (and it will). It's helpful to understand our suffering as a signal and a messenger.

The pain that you experience when a flame touches your skin is the impetus that moves your hand, protecting you from being burned. The pain of self-loss is not any different. It signals to you that something is not right, and it's this same signal that can motivate you to change your life.

I always tell my clients that during the process of healing, things often get worse before they get better. In the beginning, the more we become aware, the more it's going to hurt. It can be difficult to face the fact that our parents failed or hurt us in some way, or that we were the reason our last relationship failed. But here is the good news: Self-loss is not just a submergence into the darkness; it can also serve as a reorientation. It is a space for atonement (offering reconciliation and forgiveness to ourselves) and transformation, and ultimately our chance to *create* wholeness. It can become our opportunity for agency and freedom. Much like fire, the experience holds within itself both destruction and generative power—unapologetically molding and carving the paths of our existence.

Lost is a beautiful place in which you can feel unrestricted and uninhibited in your journey of exploring new ideas, people, meaning, and things. Lost can mark the beginning of your Self.

I have come to realize that the transformation that results from choosing to *see*, understand, and *be* who we are is unmatched by anything else. Who we are is a unique, real-time, always-evolving experience, never to be shared with a single other person. The question "Who am I?" has to be answered in the *present* moment—and it will change with every choice and exercise of our human freedom. It's important for us to realize that our task is *not* to go back and try to "find" who we used to be.

The Self is like a painting. Every moment and interaction adds paint to our canvas. The previous layers contribute to the current picture, but with every stroke, the painting changes—becomes more of what it truly is. The painting can never go back to what it once was. Your journey only moves forward. Every aspect of your life—every failure, every change, every loss, every moment of despair or joy—speaks to who you are and the life that you're living in the present moment.

Reckoning with our self-loss is a long and obscure journey—and I am here to help you with yours. The first step is to acknowledge your self-loss. It's normal to feel overwhelmed as you try to look at your Self—I mean, truly *look* at your Self. It's normal to feel exhausted or discouraged as you strive to live intentionally: *Every. Single. Day.* It's normal to buckle under the burden of responsibility that comes with recognizing your freedom to shape and *be* who you are.

The reward far outweighs the effort, though, I promise.

The reward is *you*. The real you that lives an authentic, free, and meaningful life. Note that this does *not* mean an easy, pleasant, or perfect life. This means a life where you truly experience every aspect of being alive, a life in which you fully participate, a life where you feel all of it—the excruciating and elevating moments alike. A life in which you make mistakes and emerge with lessons. A life in which you fully embody who you are.

Hard Truth

Who you are in this moment—whether you are on a plane, sitting at your kitchen table, or on your bed—IS who you really are. If you don't like who that is, it is up to you to do something about it.

Gentle Reminder

It's never too late to be you.

CHAPTER 2

What Is the Self?

It's incredibly difficult, or perhaps impossible, to discuss self-loss without understanding the concept of Self. After all, *who* is lost? *Who* are we looking for? We have all explored the concept of "Self" to one degree or another. Some of us by merely questioning who we are (even if only momentarily after a breakup, death, or other major life event), and others by experiencing a full-blown identity crisis.

This question "Who am I?" is universal; it reflects an innate need to understand our Self. Even though it's imperative to our existence, it's often asked only when we are facing challenges, transitions, despair, uncertainty, or self-loss. The truth is, most of us don't bother to go down the rabbit hole unless we've been pushed into it.

Although the "obvious" and socially promoted course of action when lost is to strive for self-discovery, what does that truly mean? Often "self-discovery" can be understood in two ways:

1. To "find" what, or who, we lost. To seek something that already exists (a Self that is formed outside our present awareness or actions). To find a Self that we are "meant" to be.

2. To discover the Self by *being* or *creating* who we are.

This dichotomy of thought is not new, and the way we understand the concept of self-discovery will depend on what we believe about the Self.

The question of Self can be dated back to the fathers of modern philosophy, Aristotle and Plato, who suggested that each person has an inherent essence—a certain set of core properties that are necessary, or *essential*, for a thing to be what it is. When a certain property is missing, this is when the essence changes and becomes a different thing. Just like a knife ceases to be a knife without a blade, we cease to be our Self when we do not exemplify certain properties. According to these early philosophers, "essentialism" means that our human task is to embody an essence that has been *given* to us. They believed that we were born to be a certain thing and we can either succeed or fail at doing so. Most of us hold this specific understanding about the Self without being aware that it stems from essentialism. And if we look closely enough, we notice that others do as well—content creators, public figures, even our friends and family. In no way did essentialism die with the early philosophers.

In response to essentialism—as the conversation in philosophy continued—existentialism emerged. Existentialism is often defined as a theory or approach that emphasizes the existence of an individual as a *free* and *responsible* agent determining their own development through acts of their will (as opposed to it being dependent on some predetermined essence). Jean-Paul Sartre, the most recognizable figure of modern-day existentialism, proposed that first we exist, and *then* we discover our essence (a view in direct opposition to essentialism). We are born and then we determine who we are through the way we *choose* to live. Sartre believed that any essence we perceive is what we have created; it was not "given" to us.

Since I am an existential psychotherapist, it's probably going to come as no surprise that I am going to use existentialism to try to answer the following two questions:

1. What is the *Self*?
2. How do we grasp it?

In order to make this philosophically heavy conversation bearable, I've done my best to provide you with a SparkNotes-esque version of the Self, rather than exhaust you with centuries' worth of theory (you're welcome!).

What I love about the existential approach is that it's filled with agency, choices, and action. Søren Kierkegaard—arguably the first existential philosopher—said that "the self is a relation that relates to itself." (If your head is spinning: Hold tight, I promise it actually means something!) The Self is defined by the way it *expresses*. Self-expression is how the Self manifests in the world and consequently constructs one's identity over time. Our understanding of who we are informs our actions, and our actions inform how we see our Self—in other words, *the Self cannot be independent of its expression.*

As a true nineties kid, I'd like to draw on a Julia Roberts movie—*Runaway Bride*—to illustrate how our actions are inextricable from our sense of Self (I mean, who says philosophical principles can't be demonstrated through lighthearted rom-coms?!). Julia's character, Maggie, has always "liked" and eaten eggs that are cooked the way her various partners enjoy. There is a scene where the main love interest, Ike (a reporter writing a story on her many failed relationships, played by Richard Gere), says to her:

IKE: You are the most lost woman I have ever laid eyes on.

MAGGIE: Lost!

IKE: That's right. You're so lost you don't even know how you like your eggs.

MAGGIE: What!?

IKE: With the priest, you liked them scrambled. With the Dead Head, fried. With the bug guy, poached. Now it's egg whites only, thank you very much.

MAGGIE: That's called changing your mind.

IKE: No, that's called not having a mind of your own.

Then, at a turning point in the movie, Maggie cooks a bunch of eggs, every which way, so that she can taste them all and decide for herself. She has finally reached the point where she wants to explore her sense of Self, including what she *actually* likes. It's a simple scene, but a powerful one. It shows that we are indeed free and responsible to figure out who we are, and sometimes that means going back to the basics and utilizing our autonomy to identify, through trial and error, how we like our proverbial eggs cooked, so that we can make and eat them with true inner consent.

The small steps are as important as any big leaps, because if our actions are scattered, our sense of Self will feel fragmented or be left undefined. It's difficult to know who we are if our behaviors are contradictory, disjointed, or inconsistent. It's like walking into a room with strobe lighting, only being able to grasp glimpses of the scene as you walk around. At no point would you get a cohesive, complete, or even accurate picture of what the room actually looks like. This is how disorienting our actions—big or small—can be.

We encounter our Self more fully by doing activities or experiencing things such as love, art, our bodies, beauty, nature, and food. We find intimacy with our Self through the closeness or oneness we have with the experience itself. The Self (self-closeness or self-intimacy) is not achieved by being isolated from the world, but rather by metaphorically tasting it, by *existing* in it.

IT'S HARD TO BE HUMAN

Not only are humans assigned the existential task of creating who we are, but, according to Sartre, this task is accompanied by "the absurdity of freedom" to do so.* Although **freedom** is something we arguably all want, we need to be aware that it demands of us to constantly make **choices** and take **responsi-**

---

* Sartre deemed existence as absurd (lacking inherent sense, value, or meaning). In other words, he believed we are left to our own devices—we are in charge of creating our own sense of Self *and* meaning in life.

bility for those choices. **Our degree of freedom will always match our degree of responsibility.**

Simply put, whenever we are free, what we choose to do (or not do) with that freedom is on us. And fortunately—or unfortunately—we are always free.* To use Sartre's words, "to be free is to be *condemned* to be free." He wasn't being dramatic; he was simply explaining that we are "condemned" because there is no respite from freedom. Which means there is no respite from responsibility for the things we do, say, or choose.

Decision-fatigue is very real, and we seek breaks without even realizing it. How often do we want someone else to choose where we will go for dinner, what movie to watch, whether we should end a relationship, post that picture on Instagram, join that pottery class, or stand up to our boss? We frequently ask people for their opinions before we've even taken the time to establish our own. Yes, it's okay to ask for advice, although, very often we are not looking for a perspective or wisdom, but rather an alleviation from the burden of constantly making decisions. I don't blame us! Decision-making is exhausting, especially given the vastness of choices many of us have the immense privilege to have. In combination with our weak or nonexistent understanding of the Self, discerning the "right" thing to do can feel overwhelming. It becomes even more burdensome once we realize the significance of each and every decision.

---

* I realize I may have just triggered many people with this statement, so please allow me to clarify: I am suggesting that we are free *within the parameters of our context* and what has been done to us—more on this later in the book, I promise.

Over the years, I've had many conversations with clients that sound like this:

> ME: Okay, so it sounds like you're aware of the changes you want to make. But where do you think the resistance is coming from?
>
> THEM: I am scared of change.
>
> ME: Ah, that makes sense. Why is change so scary for you?
>
> THEM: Because . . . what if I make the wrong choice and end up unhappy?
>
> ME: Are you happy now?
>
> THEM: No.
>
> ME: So, what's the difference?
>
> THEM: If I make a change, my unhappiness will be my fault. Now it's the context—the consequence of how life unfolded.
>
> ME: Hm. To me, it actually sounds like you're scared of responsibility, not change.
>
> THEM: I just don't want to be at fault for my own misery.
>
> ME: Unfortunately, an inaction (a lack of change) is also a decision. Even if you stay exactly as you are—that remains your responsibility.

Most of us don't want to take responsibility for not having the life we want or for not being the person we like. Instead, we avoid responsibility by surrendering our freedom. If we can blame someone for our actions, decisions, attitude, or sub-par sense of Self, we probably will (unless you're a people-pleaser, and then you take on *way* more responsibility than belongs to you . . . which is, ironically, also a form of not taking responsibility for your Self). Unfortunately, if we need proof that human beings like to avoid responsibility, we can just look at society as a whole.

Our collective avoidance of responsibility has caused and perpetrated things such as global warming, poverty, sexism, and racism (to just name a few). Also, while it may be difficult to hear, this lack of responsibility has tainted our current conversations around mental health. We've gotten carried away with labeling everyone we don't get along with as "toxic" or "narcissistic," and we've started to misuse the term "trauma" as a catchall phrase for any inconvenience that we believe now *justifies* irresponsible behavior—which is grossly unfair for all those who've experienced actual trauma.

Sartre believed that we outsource our freedom by seeking structure and direction from institutions, families, social circles, or religions—from anyone or anything—to tell us who we are or who we ought to be. For Sartre, relying on any external suggestions and structures to tell us who we are is a form of self-deception (or what he called "bad faith"). When we deceive ourselves, we start to believe or treat ourselves as if we are X (whatever we were *told* to be or whatever we feel we need to be), while deep down, a small part of us knows that we are Y.

You can fill in the blanks for yourself; what is X and what is Y for you?

To depict this point, Sartre used the analogy of a French waiter who conformed to everything a waiter "ought to be," but in his efforts, he actually appeared *too* "waiter-esque"— his exaggerated movements and behavior illustrated that he was *acting* as a waiter. His acting stripped him of who he was.

He became a thing, an object, not just in the way that others saw him but also in the way he experienced his Self.

Do you ever feel like you're acting or pretending to be your Self? Sometimes when we try to run away from the pain of nothingness, we end up self-inflicting the pain that comes from being something we are not.

Sartre stated that a common form of "bad faith" is acting as if we have no choice but to be one thing—denying one's own freedom to make one's Self into something different by choosing to change our behaviors. I see this in society all the time, when we try to eradicate our freedom by pretending it was taken away from us by an event in our past. Here is an example: We all know that one person—let's call them Brad—who was cheated on, had his heart broken in high school, or his parents got a divorce, and now he's absolutely horrible to anyone he dates in his adulthood. My question is, after validating the difficulty of that situation, at what point does his pain stop justifying the hurt he is causing? At what point does Brad need to start taking responsibility for his behavior? At what point does he need to face the fact that his choices are no longer a representation of his past hurt, but of who he has become?

Brad is not alone. The reality is, many of us don't know how to cope with our freedom, so we try to limit or escape it. We often do this by yielding to society or putting ourselves in positions that come with restrictions and parameters, allowing us to find refuge in our efforts to be who others want us to be. Most of us are comforted by certain expectations, finding meaning in our efforts to fulfill them. This perspective cannot account for every context or situation, but still, it is worth asking ourselves:

Are we surrendering our freedom because we don't want to deal with the responsibility of making choices? Are we more comfortable with someone telling us who we are than with figuring it out for ourselves?

Listen, I get it, freedom and responsibility are constant and heavy. It's an exhausting weight to carry.

There is, however, one *brief* respite we all get from our freedom (well, kind of, not really, but *please* keep reading). Kierkegaard suggested that the Self has two opposing poles: *necessity* and *possibility*. Necessities are certain concrete characteristics that we *cannot change and must work with*—such as our need for food, to be born, to die, or things that have already happened in the past—our "givens." The future, on the other hand, represents possibility. Possibility is what has *not yet happened*. This is why Kierkegaard said that we cannot look in a mirror and conclude, "Yes, there I am," because part of who we are is embodied in the possibility of all that has not yet happened. Our Self is an intersection of necessity and possibility; of the past and the future; of what we are now and what we will be.

The reason why humans can simultaneously hold necessity and possibility is that they have a unique capacity to distance themselves from what is "given" to them and acknowledge the open range of possibilities for self-definition in the future. We have the freedom to interpret and give meaning to our constraints even if we cannot escape them. For example, we cannot choose to be taller, to have a different past, birth parents, or ethnicity, or to not have a disease, but we *can* choose what meaning we make of these givens. Yes, we might have been thrown into the world without our consent, but now it's up to us to decide what to do about it. *We are responsible for how we show up every single day—in every single choice that we make—with the freedom that remains.*

Viktor Frankl—an Austrian psychiatrist and Holocaust survivor widely known for his book *Man's Search for Meaning*[*]—affirmed this idea by saying:

> Everything can be taken from a man but one thing: the last of the human freedoms—to *choose* one's attitude in any given set of circumstances, to choose one's own way.

Arguably, Frankl didn't have any basic freedoms while living as a prisoner in Nazi concentration camps during World War II. He couldn't decide when to wake up or go to bed, what to eat or wear, where to live or work. He couldn't learn a new language, visit a doctor, or hug his family. He wasn't free to leave the parameters of the concentration camp or choose whether he would live or die. He was stripped down to his final human freedom: the choice to create meaning. What's even more awe-inspiring than this recognition is that he *used* it. He used his freedom to choose his attitude, to choose his meaning, and to choose how he would approach his limited existence.

So. What's our excuse?

---

[*] It's important to note that Frankl's work extends beyond this book. He developed a psychotherapeutic modality—logotherapy—which is still practiced to this day. Although his horrific and unimaginable experiences are very different from most people's sufferings and struggles in today's world, his teachings were intended for a wide array of contexts and challenges, and go beyond just dealing with extreme suffering.

Remember, freedom does not imply that we have no constraints; freedom implies that we have a certain relationship with our "givens." Sartre said, "Freedom is what we do with what is done to us." And Frankl perfectly summarized this relationship by saying: "It is not freedom from conditions, but it *is* freedom to take a stand toward the conditions." His positioning is as firm as Sartre's—he doesn't call us condemned, but he states that human beings *are always free* (even if the freedom looks different for each circumstance).

Martin Heidegger, a German philosopher who is regarded as one of the most important philosophers of the twentieth century, similarly suggested that the *Self* (what he called *Dasein,* which translates as "being there" or "to be there") is a dynamic between who we are at this very moment and who we can and will be as time goes on. We are constantly straddling what has happened and what hasn't happened yet, and all the possibilities that remain. One could say that we *are* everything that's happened and everything that will happen. There is something liberating about knowing there is always *more* that we will become. As long as we are alive, we will never stop becoming; never stop having the ability to create our Self. It really puts our "givens" into a helpful perspective. Our past, no matter how painful, can never fully define us, because it doesn't take into account our future—that is, unless we let it.

Living through things (even difficult or painful things) and engaging with the world is what ultimately makes us . . . well, us. Our presence in the world, which includes others, is how we solidify our understanding of who we are. Our body, culture, history, and context not only shape who we are, but *are* who we are. I am *me* because of these things, not despite them.

I am unique—my essence is an intersectionality exclusive to me (in this moment).

Which is why Heidegger suggested that existing as our Selves requires something called "being-in-the-world." In German, the phrase *In-der-Welt-sein* literally translates as "being-in-the-world" (similar to his word for Self, *Dasein*— driving home the point that to exist and to be your Self cannot occur independently of each other). With that logic, it stands to reason that if we lose our Self, we cease to *be there,* we cease to exist.

No wonder losing our Self feels excruciating—like death.

THE PROBLEM OF INAUTHENTICITY

Many of us waste our life never knowing *who we are.* We constantly speak or act on behalf of the "Self," yet most of us do not know our Self intimately enough to do so. We strive for this illusive sense of "authenticity" that's been commercialized lately, but we are confused by what that means.

If you picture life as a forward motion that you cannot stop, then authenticity and inauthenticity are the same forward motion but moving in different directions. There is no neutral path, no in-between, no way to straddle the two directions. When we don't choose, take responsibility, or utilize our freedom, we are still creating a version of our Self, but it's an inauthentic one. Being inauthentic is when decisions and actions we undertake are not really our own and do not genuinely express who we understand our Self to be. To be inauthentic, according to Heidegger, is to not be an author of our own life—it's to become "unowned" or "disowned." Inauthentic behavior can be going out when you want to stay in, going along with someone's opinion even though you disagree, or choosing a job based on what your parents expect rather than what you believe is your purpose. When we disown our actions, we disown our Selves.

However, inauthenticity and self-loss are *not* the same thing. Living inauthentically is like deep-sea diving, actively swimming away from the surface but still being aware of where the surface is. Self-loss, on the other hand, is like being caught in a strong underwater current, knowing you have to swim but having no idea in which direction you should go. We are no longer aware of where the surface is, and swimming aimlessly can lead us closer to or further away from death. The *degree* of incongruence, disconnect, and disorientation that occurs in self-loss is key to distinguishing it from inauthenticity. Inauthenticity can occur when we are not paying attention, when we are not being considerate, when we are distracted or being influenced by others to turn away from the Self. It's when we do not give our Self adequate space to be, but still remain in contact with our Self. (Self-loss, on the other hand, is when this lack of space and contact becomes a permanent state of existence.)

Many of my clients who feel like they don't know who they are anymore say they feel despair. The good (or bad) news? They are not alone—we all feel despair to one extent or another when trying to face our Selves and our lives. We may feel despair for not knowing who we are (but wanting to) or for not liking who we see (and not wanting to be that person).

Most of us are either desperately trying to figure out who we are or desperately running away from the inauthentic person who we've recognized ourselves to be. Either way, we're desperate. We are all (or almost all) seeking an answer that will "solve" the mystery of the Self.

The disappointing reality is that the only concrete answer we can have about who we are is found in our own *actions*. Every day, we need to show ourselves—by being in the world—our authentic Self. How we choose to exist is up to us, but Sartre did say that the best thing we can do with our lives is to live *authentically*. And for him, authenticity meant **to accept the full weight of our freedom** (yes, yes, I'm sure you get it by now!).

THE TASK OF AUTHENTICITY

To summarize thus far, the Self entails three key ingredients: freedom, choice, and responsibility. *We create our sense of Self with the choices we make, the sense of responsibility with which we approach our existence, and the way we use our freedom despite our constraints.*

It's taken me a while to come to a place where I find this premise empowering. This perspective is hard and uncomfortable, and I used to be seriously triggered by it. It's similar to that feeling we get the first time people treat us as an adult. When someone has the audacity to tell us to make our own choices or take responsibility for our mistakes. *How dare they?* I remember thinking. *What? I am supposed to just, like, adult now, all on my own? I shouldn't be allowed to be in charge of myself!*

The icing of this triple-layered existential cake (which I'm guessing might be tasting a bit too dense right now) is that although freedom is always there presenting us with choices, *no one* can tell us what to do with it. Whatever we choose to do, or not do, *we* are responsible for.

Here is an example Sartre shared: A man came to him asking for help in making a decision. He had to choose to go fight in the war he believed in (although his role would probably be small) or stay and take care of his elderly mother who was all alone (and be a big part in a small cause). Sartre stated that no one could help him find the "right" answer because there is no right answer *until* the man chose one. *The right answer is an authentic answer, and no one else could lead him to the decision that was truly authentic.* So, his choice—no matter what it was—was the only *true* choice.

"Authenticity" really is the word du jour in modern culture. Which is lovely, except somewhere along the way to making it trendy, we've managed to strip it of its weight and meaning. The word "authentic" has been grossly misused, overused, and watered down in an effort to make it more accessible. So, to try to avoid confusion going forward, let's explore what I mean by authenticity.

To say something is authentic is to say that something *is* what it professes to be, what it is believed to be, or that it represents what it truly is. But we cannot talk about human authenticity without talking about the Self. Does being authentic mean being one's Self? Does it mean being at one with one's Self? Or, does it mean representing one's Self?

In the framework of existential analysis, I understand authenticity as finding peace and a center within ourselves. Authenticity is a space where our doubting ends and we feel grounded, like we have hit the depth within (inner resonance).

It's the deep, intuitive feeling (sense) of rightness of our being (*Dasein*). It is when we can finally say *yes* to who we are (offer inner consent in any given moment). The essence of who we are can only come through attunement, and attunement is only possible through intimate knowing. Just like we can't know the message of a song unless we listen to the lyrics, we can only know our Self by paying attention. So tune in. Try *all* the eggs.

Authenticity is having a sense of Self that says: *This is me, in this moment, this is how I want to be.*

Today, people often use authenticity as a scapegoat. When someone's action is followed by a declaration in the vein of "I am just being authentic," they are usually looking to be relieved of their responsibility for something they just said or did. It's a misuse of the word, though, because *to be authentic is to be responsible and own your choices*. But we often shy away from this particular thought, because when we are hurting, when things are hard or unfair, we want to believe that we are absolved of our responsibility for *how* we show up in the world. This is often when we misuse our freedom and jeopardize our authenticity.

The common concept of "authenticity" comes to us mainly from Heidegger's 1927 book *Being and Time*. He coined a new word, *Eigentlichkeit*. When translated, this German word literally means "own-ness" or "being owned" or being "one's own"; and because we are free and responsible, authenticity could be understood as owning what we do and who we are at every unique intersection of existence (from moment to moment). It's what makes us irreplaceable, irreducible, unrepeatable. Sartre said:

There is no doubt that I could have done otherwise, but that is not the problem. It ought to be formulated like this: Could I have done otherwise without perceptibly modifying the organic totality of the projects that make up who I am?

Every action modifies the totality of who we are. In other words, when we change our actions, we change our sense of Self.

A dear friend of mine and I were recently talking about self-loss over coffee (fun!) and they asked me, "If some people lose their sense of Self, and some have never formed a sense of Self to begin with, does this mean that some people must *reestablish* their Self?" It was a thought-provoking question. I sat with it for a minute and then answered: "*No.* Everyone establishes a sense of Self, constantly. From moment to moment, your Self perpetually changes—is constantly becoming—therefore it cannot be *re*-established."

Figuring out "who I am" requires an attitude of understanding that I am, in essence, "unfathomable."* Simply put, this means that the person we are will continue to change and evolve.

The beautiful (and possibly frustrating) thing about being human? *We are impossible to pin down.*

Our ultimate essence is always "ahead" of us, and we will never completely *be* it. People are often overwhelmed by this

---

* I love this word, "unfathomable," as a means of describing our human essence! It's humbling and hopeful all at the same time—at least that's how I felt when I first heard this description during my existential analysis training.

fact. Most of us are hoping for a onetime "journey" of discovery, rather than a lifetime of responsibility. Yet the Self is not a prize or a mere possession. We don't have the privilege of staring at our Self and preserving its beauty, wholeness, and integrity regardless of how we live our lives. How we live changes *us*.

And, even with all these changes, I see the Self as consistent. This is because I understand consistency as our ability to show up in alignment with what we believe in and how we see our Selves over and over again. This belief makes me feel safe. I also find safety and strength in the Self's flexibility, movement, and malleability.

Think about it like this: It's possible to shatter a rock, and impossible to break water. Many people's idea of the Self is like a rock. Something that must be formed, "set," and unmovable. And yet, the Self is more like water—flowing, changing, navigating around the things in its path. Your fluidity is your power, not your weakness.

Here is a challenge: Pick a day this week and, for its entirety, really behave in a way that aligns with how you understand your Self. Approach the day as if every single little (or big) decision and act matters (what kind of coffee you'll order, what your posture will look like, the words you will choose to speak, what kind of eggs you'll eat). Fill each and every moment with intent, and keep checking in. Look for the feeling of resonance when you are aligned, congruent, at peace— when things feel right and "at home" within yourself. Remember, if being true to your Self is new for you, it may feel strange, awkward, or uncomfortable at first. Accept the discomfort of trying something different and give it time.

THE ACT OF BECOMING

It's important for me to acknowledge that my own under-standing of what it means to *be* human has been heavily influ-enced by my professor Alfried Längle—psychotherapist, psychiatrist, psychologist, former founder and president of the International Society for Logotherapy and Existential Analy-sis, and former vice president of the worldwide International Federation of Psychotherapy (the oldest such institution). Län-gle was a pupil of—and collaborated closely with—Viktor Frankl.* And, did you know that Frankl knew Martin Hei-degger?! The fact that I get to partake in this lineage by calling Längle not just my doctoral supervisor, but my mentor, has been one of my life's greatest honors. His teachings were my springboard into existential philosophy and psychotherapy, and have heavily informed this book and my understanding of what it means to be one's Self, as well as what it means to be lost. You will find that I mention Längle a lot—and I mean a *lot*—throughout the book, and that's because this book wouldn't exist without him!

It should also come as no surprise that his theory of exis-tential analysis was the inspiration for my first tattoo, which I got during one of the lowest points in my life (just before the panic attack). The tattoo is simple, a single word: *Être*. It's the French verb "to be." At that time, I wanted to remind myself to *exist*—change, choose, transform, transcend, be my Self in

---

* Over time, the two diverged theoretically due to Längle's new develop-ment in the field of existential analysis.

each and every moment—rather than to merely survive. I wanted to mark my body with something that would represent the intersection of my past and future (which I still didn't know how to navigate). I wanted to give myself permission to be my Self. I wanted to remember that each moment and each decision allows me to shape who I am. I wanted all of this, even while in the depths of my loss.

I guess I wanted something that I never had: my Self. Today, the art of *being* and *becoming* is more central to how I live my life. It's my anchor, orientation, and, dare I say, my *philosophy* of life.

How we understand life is how we live it. How we understand the Self is how we *be(come)* it. So, here are some questions that can help you begin the process of understanding your relationship with your Self.

Do you seek an essence that you believe has been given to you by someone else (a North Star you are meant to follow), or do you believe that it's up to you to mold, shape, and create your essence with your choices? Are you a detective or an artist? An archaeologist or an architect?

Self
- What is your definition of Self?
- How would you describe your Self in fifty words? (Yes, fifty!)
- How do you define authenticity?
- What "givens" and possibilities do you see in your life?

RESPONSIBILITY

- What were you taught about responsibility?
- How do you define responsibility?
- What do you feel responsible for?
- What do you *not* feel responsible for?
- Do you take responsibility for the current version of you? Why or why not?
- Do you think the responsibility for who you are should be shared with others? If yes, with whom?

CHOICES

- What have you been taught about making choices?
- What choices are you avoiding making in your life right now?
- What decisions are the hardest for you to make?
- What scares you the most about making a choice?
- What have you been choosing, but want to stop?

FREEDOM

- What have you been taught about freedom?
- How do you define freedom?
- Do you feel free to be your Self?
- What do you think is limiting your freedom?
- Do you feel anxious about being free?
- What are some things you have freedom over?

There are a lot of quotes out there about trusting that you are exactly where and who you need to be. And, although they feel good to read, they often don't actually represent our reality. Maybe you are *not* where or who you want to be.

If you were to keep living your life exactly as you are in this very moment, will it be enough? When you are on your death-bed will you be able to say to yourself, "That was a life well lived"?

I don't mean to convey that the trick here is to view your sense of Self as a pass/fail exam, but rather that you should embrace it as your life's task. Your Self is your ultimate mas-terpiece.

Summary of Terms

In order to help solidify some of the complex ideas we've dis-cussed, here is a little existential glossary:*

1. **Authenticity.** Authenticity is not your given or precon-ceived nature (although that sounds lovely); rather, au-thenticity is the process of *deciding and creating* who you are. It is existing in congruence with your actions, feel-ings, and thoughts. We "uncover" who we are, but we un-cover it by *creating* who we become. Authenticity is a way of existing that is achieved by accepting the burden of re-sponsibility, choice, and freedom. Authenticity requires participation.

2. **Freedom.** Freedom is the ability that you have to make de-cisions. You can say *yes* or, alternatively, you can say *no*. You have the power of choice, independent of force or dependency. Yes, this can be a daunting concept for many, but my stance remains—we always have freedom of

---

* This glossary is based on the existential analysis theory with my own in-terpretations and tweaks.

choice. In most contexts we are free to act, and in some extreme and oppressive circumstances, we are left with only the freedom to create meaning.

3. **Responsibility.** Responsibility is taking ownership of your decisions and actions. *You* are the author of your life. Your existence always comes back to you. All that you are is connected to a world that constantly asks you to engage with it. You are asked to respond, so you are responsible.

4. **Meaning.** To search for meaning is to see and understand what something is—or what you are—here for. It is finding purpose and value in your experiences. Instead of asking, "What should I ask of life?" re-center by asking, "What is life asking of me?"

Hard Truth

You are always free, which means that you are always responsible.

Gentle Reminder

Who you are will evolve and change; allow it.

CHAPTER 3

What Is Life Asking of Me?

A favorite professor in one of my undergraduate courses started our moral philosophy class by recounting a story. He explained that for the past twenty years the final exam for the class consisted of a one-word question: "Why?" The time he gave for his exams was notoriously long—varying from three to eight hours (he would hand out entire notebooks to allow for the space most people needed to answer the question). Students usually showed up with snacks, water bottles, and multiple pens. He was known to rarely give out A's and never A-pluses (he believed there was always room for growth). Well, that is until one person finally got it right.

To everyone's shock, he explained that, last year, a student completed the test in five minutes. They walked up to the professor's desk, handed in their notebook, and walked out of the classroom. The professor was puzzled. He turned to the first page of the student's notebook and found their two-word answer:

Why not?

Most of us want a concrete answer to why we are alive, why life is worth living, and why we should bother or not bother being our Self. This plucky young existentialist-in-the-making challenged the premise that there would be a right or wrong answer (or an answer at all). Instead, he leaned into the vastness of possibility.

Meaning is perhaps the topic where existential philosophers and existential therapists diverge the most. When I tell people I am an existential therapist, they often understand the two words separately but have a hard time putting them together. How could someone who presumably believes in the meaninglessness and absurdity of life help others make sense of their own?

Early on in sessions, most of my clients who feel lost want to know exactly *how* they will figure out who they are, as if therapy can box up all the answers and hand-deliver them wrapped up in a bow (oh, how I wish!). They want to *know* the tangible steps, they want to be given a map that will show them exactly what the process of being their Self will look like. Having things structured and easily anticipated often makes people feel safe and hopeful—I get it. But when you choose to work with me, we end up focusing on the "why" as much as the "how" of the equation, because the why will ultimately dictate the how. As Nietzsche said, "If you have your why for life, you can get by with almost any how." Determining *why* you want to live will help you know *how* you want to live, which will in turn shape *who you are*. Meaning is not just the cherry on top of the cake, it's the batter.

It's no coincidence that existentialism came into its own after World War II, when life and the atrocities of the Holocaust challenged everyone's understanding of the world being an orderly and meaningful place. However, meaning is the very thing that kept Frankl alive, and so he proposed that striving to find meaning is our primary motivational force in life (rather than pleasure or power).

Längle considers meaning to be one of the four fundamental motivations needed to live a *truly* fulfilling life (so, it's really important!).

Take a moment and reflect on the following questions. Can you give a wholehearted "yes"—your inner consent—to all four?

1. **I am here; but can I truly *be*? Can I exist?**
   Am I privy to conditions and context that offer me safety, support, space, and protection? Do I trust myself and the world around me? Am I provided with basic human needs that allow me to live? Can I accept my conditions?

2. **I am alive, but do I like it?**[*]
   Does the way I live my life nurture a connection with my values and the people around me? Do I like the fact that I am alive? Can I connect to the way I feel and to those around me? Am I moved—*touched*—by life?

---

[*] Although Frankl managed to find meaning even in the concentration camps, no one would argue that he had a *wholly* fulfilling existence. I don't imagine he could have always answered *yes* to this question.

3. **Can I be myself?**

   Do I feel like I have the *right* to be who I am? Do I have permission (from Self and others) and space to be and express myself?

4. **Do I have meaning in life?**

   What is my direction and purpose in life? Can I identify why I am alive and how I want to exist while I am?

As you may have noticed, the final condition listed—although arguably the first condition proposed—is *meaning*. Without meaning, **our existence will not be fulfilled.** Without tackling the *why*, we simply cannot fully exist.

Let's take a moment to expand on what I mean by existence:

- Existence is being in the here-and-now; being present, alive, and creative.
- Existence is being engaged with life.
- Existence is experiencing everything (the joy and the suffering alike).
- Existence is a stance that says, "I am open to what is there."
- Existence is our implementation of the will.
- Existence is living with inner consent.
- Existence is action.
- Existence is both a gift and a task. Existence is a choice.
- Existence is stepping out and rising above our conditions.
- Existence is our freedom to *be* or not to *be* (and isn't that *the* question?).*

---

* List based on Existential Analysis training material.

Ultimately, existence means to create something out of one's Being. And one could argue that truly existing is what makes life meaningful. Meaning is our **participation in and orientation toward** being alive. If we do not participate in life and have no clear direction of where we are going, our life is stripped down to the basic functions of breathing and having a beating heart (and it's extremely difficult to find meaning in that state).

MEANING AND TIME

Our time on earth is limited, and this one simple fact threatens our Self. We can get anxious thinking about the reality that we have a ticking clock associated with our ability to exist and make our lives mean something. This is normal. Meaning emerges from time—but it is not constrained by time. Meaningful actions are what occur when we participate in life with a full awareness of its finiteness. Although time brings with it an awareness of death, it also motivates us to recognize and own each unique moment and make it count (#YOLO, if you will). And, of course, the opposite is true: An infinite amount of time can cause complacency and meaninglessness.

The only way humans can face life without despair is by living it meaningfully.

It's always fascinating to me when I ask friends how their life would change if they knew they only had three months to live (yes, I am that fun friend that asks things like that at dinner parties). The life—and Self—they often describe is one very different from their own. An existence they would rather have, and would find worthy or meaningful enough to take up their precious time (a Self that spends more time with family, travel, skydiving, living out of a van and driving across the country, applying to a grad school program, volunteering, etc.). But why are they not working toward living a version of that life *now*? Why is avoiding the risk and effort—playing it safe, so to speak—deemed more important than an invigorating, fulfilling life? Why do they resist that version of their Self, just because they think they have all the time in the world? I mean, I get it, of course. I still struggle not to do the same. But I have discovered that I want to live a life, and be the person, that means something to me. And now I try, every day, to move in that direction. It isn't always easy, or even enjoyable, to live like this—to stay attuned (all the freakin' time) or make decisions that respect who I am. To be awake instead of blissfully sleepwalking—but it has *always* felt like it holds value. It *always* feels true. And there is infinite beauty, and profound satisfaction, in that.

Whenever I lose the sense that time is finite, I often notice that my sense of meaning gets lost, too. Many of my relationships have been long-distance, and I've discovered that when my partner and I are together, the closer we get to the time of separation, the nicer and more attentive we become with each other. Knowing that our time together has to end helps us make the days we have more intentional and special. When we start to take time for granted, we take each other for granted.

So, instead of feeling trampled by time, I've learned to *use* it.

WHERE DOES MEANING COME FROM?

So, how do we figure out our meaning? Many approach the question by asking, "What is the meaning of life?" But this is unanswerable, vague, and abstract, and we get stuck in it. Frankl compared it to asking a chess champion, "Tell me, Master, what is the best move in the world?" There is no one "best move," because the circumstances are different in every single match, for every single person. An existential therapist could not tell you what the "meaning of life" is any more than a chess master could tell you what the single "best move" is.

In most narratives I hear, implicit in the idea of "finding meaning" is the assumption that this is a thing we do *once* and that it comes from something much "bigger than us" (translation: *It's out of our control*). We find meaning only because it's been "given" to us to find. This usually aligns with the concept that the universe, a higher power, or an energy life force offers meaning that we are asked to embrace. I know it *sounds* idyllic, but what happens when what we are taught or have been "given" doesn't align with who we understand our Self to be? For example, what if you are gay but were told that meaning comes from marriage between a man and a woman, or if you know you don't want children but were told that you'd never know happiness until you procreated?

The thing is, I can't tell you where you should (or shouldn't) derive your meaning from, but I *can* offer an additional perspective: What if we are responsible for *creating* (by *living*) our meaning rather than merely *finding* it?

What if meaning can be found in the act of creating it, according to your unique life and to what resonates? This existential principle can even apply to people who practice a religion. For example, being Christian is not just about your internal faith, it's also about the *way* you live your life. The way to embrace any meaning is to live it. However, keep in mind that it's not solely the *action* that is meaningful. Oftentimes, we conflate meaning with productivity (and believe me, the two don't always go hand in hand). Society today has made us feel that if we're not being *productive*, we are wasting our time, we are not valuable. But I think we all know that it's possible to be "successful" or "busy" without having *any* sense of meaning. If our actions hold no value, inner consent, active intention, or attunement, the outcome itself is meaningless—it adds up to nothing. And if we focus *only* on our personal productivity, plans, and to-do lists, we are devaluating the world, because it has just become a tool to live out our desires. On the other hand, if we solely focus on the world and not our Self, we lose our Self. And if we lose our Self, there is, of course, no meaning to our existence.

Is this sounding a little grim? I promise it's ultimately not, but I do need to stress that it is a delicate balancing act. Maybe a more approachable way to look at meaning is by acknowledging that each one of us has our own specific mission that we get to carry out. Everyone's task is distinctive to their opportunity and context. Meaning will be different for each individual, and it may differ from day to day or moment to moment. In his book, Frankl writes, "What matters, therefore, is not the meaning of life in general but rather the specific meaning of a person's life at a given moment." Simply, we need to acknowledge meaning in *everything* we do. Meaning speaks to every action—about what we are doing *right now* (e.g., drawing with your kid, making dinner, reading this book, talking to friends, sending a text or email). And actions create who the Self is in any given moment.

Here's what I'm getting at: *Small, meaningful decisions reveal who we are more than big existential questions.*

Do you remember the last time you felt a perfect, meaningful moment? For me, it was lying on the sand beneath the stars in Wadi Rum (the red desert in Jordan). The temperature was ideal, the sand supporting my body was soft, and the sky was filled with unquantifiable vastness and majesty, illuminated by stars. My life suddenly felt small (in comparison to the vastness above me), but still important—I understood that I was part of the greater tapestry of existence. I recognized that I am a valuable part of a picture I cannot even fully see—one much, *much* bigger than me.

If you feel like you've lost your meaning along the way, it could be helpful to think about the last time you experienced it. Was it laughing with friends? Looking out at the ocean? Singing your child to sleep? It's important to be curious about how you feel toward the different areas of your life. It's easy to conflate our lack of meaningfulness in one area with the way we perceive life as a whole, but let's not do that. We can feel unfulfilled at our job, but still have a fulfilling life. But, if we let it, our discontentment can become all-consuming. If you are facing a sense of meaninglessness, it may mean you are orienting your life in the wrong direction. Our meaning of life may shift and change, but it never ceases to *be*.

So, instead of asking, "What meaning can life offer me?"

let's reframe the question as *"What is life asking of me?"*[*] Then, we get to *choose* how we respond. Meaning is an *act of devotion* in response to life's questions—an ongoing process to understand the world and take responsibility for the way we choose to be in it. It's how we choose to take care of our Selves, others, our society, and our planet.

Frankl proposes that we can discover this meaning in life in three different ways:

- By creating a work or doing a deed
- By experiencing something or encountering someone
- Through the attitude we take toward unavoidable suffering

Let's be clear: Frankl is not advocating that we can only experience meaning in suffering, but rather that we can *still* find meaning *while* we are suffering. There are contexts and circumstances that we cannot change, and yet we are still responsible for choosing to live a meaningful life: "When we are no longer able to change the situation, we are challenged to change ourselves."

Have you ever done something that was really unpleasant, painful, or hard, but that you *had* to do? Maybe you stood up for someone who was being bullied or mistreated? Maybe you endured the pain of labor in order to bring your child into this world? Was it easier once there was a meaning attached to it?

---

[*] This is a powerful reframing I learned during my training. It helped me pay attention to the bigger picture of life and understand my part within it. It also helped me feel empowered. I finally realized that I had the freedom to choose my answer.

Frankl once gave an example of an elderly man whose wife passed away. He was inconsolable until he came to a realization that the fact that he was suffering meant that she *didn't* have to suffer *his* death. This suffering, or sacrifice, then had meaning, and was easier for him to bear. Similarly, I see individuals who go through divorce and whose hurt is unbearable until they ground in the fact that this will benefit their children.

Although we often approach meaning very cognitively, it's important to know that it's accessible intuitively. In fact, for the most part, meaning happens *outside* our cognitive awareness. This is why most people don't ask the question of meaning explicitly (unless they experience trauma, a big transition, self-loss, etc.); it's often intuitive and something they *live*.

DO YOU HAVE SOMETHING TO LIVE FOR?

During my first semester of graduate school, I was taking an Introduction to Counseling class that gave an overview of all the prominent therapeutic modalities. To be honest, I have very little recollection of what was in the "existential therapy" chapter, but one thing caught my attention and sticks out in my mind to this day: a brief transcript of a conversation between a therapist and a suicidal client who was expressing all the reasons they wanted to die.

After hearing what the client had to say, the therapist retorted with a simple question: "Okay then, why don't you kill yourself?"

Wait, what? My jaw dropped. *We are allowed to say that?* I was horrified, thrilled, stunned, and delighted. This very line is what sparked my interest in existential therapy. Many classmates found this approach provocative (it is) and insensitive. But I found it poignant and raw. Fyodor Dostoyevsky—my favorite Russian novelist (and existentialist)—wrote: "For the secret of men's being is not only to live but to have something to live for." What this therapist was asking, albeit in a very confrontational way, was ultimately *Do you have something to live for?* Their question got me thinking.

Everyone should have a choice whether they live or die; but a life without meaning is, well, meaningless. Unless we know *why* we are *choosing* to live—what to dedicate our Self to—life has essentially ended. *Reintroducing meaning is the only way to actually save a life.* However, reintroduction is not the same thing as indoctrination—it's not about telling someone what to believe in; it's about getting the individual to face their own meaninglessness and take responsibility for it.

Frankl talks about a client who asked him to differentiate between logotherapy—a therapy that focuses "on the meaning of human existence as well as on man's search for such a meaning"—and psychoanalysis (the Freudian approach).

Before he answered, Frankl first asked the client to define how he understood psychoanalysis, to which the client said:

"During psychoanalysis, the patient must lie down on a couch and tell you things which sometimes are disagreeable to tell."

Then Frankl replied to him: "Now, in logotherapy the patient may remain sitting erect, but he must hear things which sometimes are very disagreeable to hear."

Although his comment comes off cheeky, I do believe that Frankl's response encapsulates how difficult it can be to face existential questions. I have found that many people are not merely scared of the task of finding the "answer," they are too scared to even ask the question. I am here to tell you that if you don't know what your meaning is or why you are alive, *it's okay*! It is not pathological, it's simply existential angst. Distress is not a bad thing, it's the *tension* that gives our existence shape, and we have to learn to lean into it, to embrace it. We are perpetually caught between what we have done and what we want to accomplish—*this* is the meaningful act of becoming one's Self. Frankl explains this idea:

> I consider it a dangerous misconception of mental hygiene to assume that what man needs in the first place is equilibrium or, as it is called in biology, "homeostasis." What a man actually needs is not a tensionless state but rather the striving and struggling for a worthwhile goal, a freely chosen task. What he needs is not the discharge of tension at any cost but the call of potential meaning waiting to be fulfilled by him.

I sit with the tension of my existence almost on a daily basis. Some days it feels like a gentle check-in, and other days it feels like a heavy burden. Just the other day, I was writing in a coffee shop, and I began to quietly scrutinize the meaning of life. It hit me that we really don't have much time here, and what was the point of it all, anyway? Was I doing the right thing with my life? Did my work with clients or on Instagram ultimately matter? What was the point of relationships if they all ultimately end with death? Why was I so convinced there was a reason to wake up tomorrow? Slowly, my food started to taste bland, the words I was writing felt empty, and I stared aimlessly out the window. *Cue a black-and-white filter with some moody piano music in the background.*

But this tension didn't feel threatening to who I was nor to my existence (trust me, it has in the past), because I am at a place in my life where I feel grounded in my Self. Now moments like this have become informational and meaningful—sometimes profound. I have surrendered to the difficulty and frequency of these questions, and instead of throwing me into a darkness, these uncomfortable moments help me reorient and ensure that I remain an active participant in my own fulfillment. They keep me on my toes, so to speak. And so I value them.

But this wasn't the case for me for a long time, and it's not the reality for many. I used to be haunted by my inner disorientation and emptiness; it used to be so uncomfortable that I wanted to do anything to escape it. I felt a strong void within myself, and in a sloppy search for meaning, I placed things that didn't belong into that void, impulsively trying to numb the pain with a stream of relationships (of all types), recognition for accomplishments, and countless mind-numbing hours watching TV. In an ironic twist, it was the process of exploring that void—the messy unraveling of my own self-loss—that gave me the meaning I was lacking all along. The very first step was figuring out how the fuck I got to a place where "Who am I?" was a question I had no clue how to answer.

Hard Truth

A meaningful life begins when you decide your life is worth living.

Gentle Reminder

Ground in your why and it will lead you to your how.
Be true to your how and it will lead you to your Self.

PART II

The Self You Lost

The world will ask you who you are, and if you don't know, the world will tell you.

—CARL JUNG

CHAPTER 4

What Causes Self-Loss?

There are two types of people in this world: those who had a sense of Self and then lost it, and those who *never* got to understand, or be, their true Self. It can be hard to discern into which category we fall; and, ultimately, it's irrelevant. Once we are lost, the discomfort and consequences feel the same. In both circumstances, we are presented with the difficult task of facing our loss, and tracing back to its origin: *When, how, and why did it happen?* Embodiment—the unifying of Self—won't come from simply mining the past, but looking back can allow us to gain perspective, compassion, and meaningful lessons that will help shape our future.

For me, the process of self-loss began at a young age. If I had to pick an exact moment, it would be when I was nine years old, the first night I spent in a bomb shelter.

I remember that night vividly, because it was in such stark contrast to the peaceful day that preceded it. Apart from the uncharacteristically sunny weather and my stroll to the town square where I got my first ice cream of the season, the spring afternoon was perfectly normal—well, at least what was considered normal for what was formerly known as Yugoslavia in 1999. In the months leading up, all public spaces in my small town teemed with whispers, profanities, desperate prayers that sounded a lot like bargaining, and most important, speculations of war.

That evening, my entire family was sprawled across the living room couch to watch our weekly episode of *Esmeralda*, a Mexican telenovela that we never missed. Just a few minutes into the show, the TV let out a long, high-pitched whine that changed the scene into a sequence of colorful lines. Across the screen, a declaration of WAR appeared in big bold letters. I struggle to remember the specifics of the announcement, but the final sentence can roughly be translated into: "The war has begun." Moments later, the sounds of air-raid sirens wailed. We were under attack. And in that moment, my childhood ended.

We rushed outside to run to an underground cellar that was located next door. It was the only shelter we could think of. Just as we stepped onto the cobblestone street, there was a deafening sound. As we looked in the direction of the explosion, we saw a large orange cloud of fire. It took less than a second to feel the rush of hot air. The first bomb had landed, only a few kilometers from us.

I stood frozen. Unfamiliar with any emotion that could match the experience, I did—and felt—absolutely nothing.

In the days following, my family sought refuge in public bunkers—underground structures filled with hundreds of people (strangers). The spaces were lit with flickering fluorescent lights, the floors covered with ripped blankets and old mattresses. The air was filled with thick smoke from cigarettes.

We lived like this for a couple of months, and I am not sure exactly at what moment it happened, but ultimately the trauma of war shifted my priority from self-awareness to self-preservation. Our only concerns became having enough food, bomb-proofing our house, being ready to run at a moment's notice (sleeping in shifts, in our clothing, with go-bags next to us), finding space in bunkers, and figuring out ways for my family to escape the former Yugoslavia (one by one, and separately). But little did I know that the escape would be even more traumatic than the captivity itself.

I remember holding hands with my mom as we crossed the bridge to the bus terminal. Before we made it halfway across, the air-raid sirens went off. Within seconds, we saw a plane flying straight toward us. We began to run as fast as we could. When I think of this moment, I can still feel my heart beating in my chest. There was no reality in which we could have outrun the plane, but luckily it took a turn and bombed a different bridge that day. At the bus terminal, breathless and shaking, I said goodbye to my mom and, clutching a plastic bag full of snacks, got on a bus to Bosnia by myself. I had no idea who would pick me up on the other side or where exactly I was going.

For a long time, I didn't want to admit to myself that these experiences fundamentally changed me. Such a realization felt like a defeat; I didn't want to give the enforcers of war anything more than the many lives they had already taken. But the truth always comes out eventually, doesn't it?

Although the crisis ended, and my family immigrated to Canada, I remained living in survival mode into my early twenties. For me, that looked like self-protecting by being judgmental, shut-down, and untrusting of others. When you feel like your existence is perpetually threatened, you don't allow yourself to do anything but survive—and you guard yourself at all costs. My trauma warped my sense of reality and stripped me of my agency. *Or so I thought.*

Have you ever heard the story of the elephant and the rope? It's been said that a baby elephant can be trained by having its front leg tied to a stake with a thin rope. At first the elephant will struggle to break free, but eventually it learns that it can't. Once the elephant grows, it stops trying to tug the rope or uproot the stake because it has been conditioned to believe that it's not possible. The elephant remains captured, even though it now has enough strength to set itself free. What once constrained it no longer has the power to do so, yet the elephant is unaware.

I was the elephant. I was truly helpless as a child amid a war, but I wasn't helpless as an adult living a life that I didn't want—yet, I couldn't distinguish the difference. Part of healing was realizing that it was safe enough to *be;* to show up as my Self. That I had agency, even power. That what I felt, thought, wanted, and needed actually *mattered.* That who I am was not merely a consequence of painful life events, but rather a cumulation of decisions that shape who I become. That the only threat present was from my self-loss.

Until I reached this awareness—and consequently began to approach life differently—I could not give my inner consent to the life I was performing. (I don't want to say "living," because living implies being honest and grounded in reality, and I wasn't.) *My awareness is what set me free.* Well, actually, my *actions* set me free, but they were informed by the awareness. Awareness is where it all starts. This was a difficult task, given that the people closest to me survived the same traumatic events and normalized them to such an extent that it took until my early twenties for me to realize that it was, in fact, trauma.

At some point, we *must* open our eyes to what has happened to us and admit to ourselves all that we've done. Awareness is rarely stumbled upon; if we want deeper insight into our self-loss, we need to be deliberate and intentional as we explore and face the experiences that have caused it, as well as our actions that have perpetuated and kept us imprisoned by it.

CAUSES OF SELF-LOSS

Although responsibility seems to be an inescapable theme when talking about self-loss, I want to validate the fact that self-loss *always* comes with a reason, a trigger, a cause. No one wakes up one day and relinquishes their Self. Well, not intentionally anyway. Regardless of whether it's an obstacle that hindered our ability to truly identify and live our authentic Self in the first place, or something that severed or eroded our connection over time, in my clinical work I have found the following three causes of self-loss to be the most common:

1. Life-altering events
2. Modeled behavior and family rules
3. Self-betrayal

Life-Altering Events

Certain events modify the relationship we have with our Self because they present a barrier or hurdle to understanding or embodying who we are. Following such life-altering events, one of three things often occurs:

1. We begin to self-identify with the pain/event.
2. We struggle to reconcile who we were prior to the event with who we are now.
3. We experience mental health struggles that make us feel less connected to, or ashamed of, ourselves.

There is no hard-and-fast rule for what such events may look like. Two people can experience the exact same thing and be impacted differently.

Although my childhood trauma echoed through to my adulthood, would you believe that the pressure and struggle I experienced in my early twenties was far more painful than surviving a war? It was. Most people are surprised to hear me say that. The truth is, it doesn't matter *what* we have lived through—or how big or small others deem it to be—we cannot evaluate or judge an event itself without understanding its impact. For me the event that initially triggered my self-loss was the war, and later, what deepened and perpetuated this loss was getting married before I was ready (and to the wrong person); for others, it's geographical relocation, a medical diagnosis, the loss of a loved one, a relationship setback, or having a child (just to name a few).

Any event can be significant enough to halt, distort, or hinder our relationship with our Self. Meaning, such events make it more difficult for us to act, feel, and/or decide in accordance with who we understand our Self to be.

I once worked with a man who found out that his wife had been having an affair. Handling infidelity is difficult enough on its own, but what made it feel all-consuming was that he had made the relationship—his role as a husband and father—the center of his entire Self. As a consequence, when he saw his wife with another man, his sense of self completely shattered:*

"I was lost because the entire framework for the plan of getting married and having a family and progressing with children—the rug—was pulled out from under me. The framework was collapsing and I didn't have an alternative to compensate for that loss. So I was bewildered, annoyed, and angry at the betrayal . . . but also worried: *Well, what does this mean?*

"I remember, I just laid on the bed and I was *screaming* to get it out of my system 'cause I knew my life was destroyed . . . or, I thought so at the time. I am not sure I had much sense of myself. I can remember feeling [*long pause*] . . . completely leaden . . . just *dead*. I felt like it was all *over*."

Even decades *after* discovering his wife's infidelity, he continued to self-identify with his pain. He didn't embrace the possibilities he may have had for the future, he stayed stuck in

---

* All the quotes in this chapter are transcribed verbatim from interviews I conducted during my MA research on moral injury; one of the themes I studied was self-estrangement.

his limitations, or "givens." And as a result, he had no connection to his Self. His pain became his identity.

> "The facts are, and my life experiences are, that I am a victim. I was taken advantage of, and I was foolish in how I allowed that to happen. I am a naïve *fool*. Even though I am in my late sixties, I look back over the years at the various relationships and choices and behaviors and in particular in the last ten, twelve . . . [*sigh*] and I chide myself for being a fool."

Although certain events may take away a role that has become an important part of how we experience our Self, in other contexts—such as becoming a parent—we are given a new role. For some, this transition may feel like a natural addition to who they are, while for others it feels like an intrusion— endless acts revolving around a role that does not resonate with how they think, feel, or experience themselves. It can be difficult for some people to reconcile who they are now with who they were before having a child.

Recently, I was scrolling on TikTok and saw a video where a woman said something like, "I'm so sick of people saying that being a mother is not a personality." She went on to say that since she had her child (nine months ago), everything she's done has been for them. She said she'd done nothing that was solely for her Self. So how could being a mother *not* be her personality? I get it; for her, motherhood was all she felt she had in that moment in time. It was the only way she could understand her Self, probably because her day-to-day actions reflected only motherhood back to her. And it can be incredibly difficult to differentiate our *role* from our *identity*. Identity is who we are; roles are what we do. But, of course, what we do informs our identity. It's all connected. For mothers, it can be challenging to identify a Self outside of that specific role. This inability to see or recognize our Self in our actions can feel scary, overwhelming, and is experienced as a loss for many. Others, on the other hand, may feel relieved or fulfilled by motherhood—they've been given something that offers them meaning and an opportunity to express their Self in a new way.

A woman I worked with spoke about the harsh reality and loss of Self she encountered as a consequence of *cheating on her partner*:

"I feel that the experience [of infidelity] shook me to the core, getting me to realize how fallible I was. And that I wasn't perfect. And that I wasn't as good as everybody thought I was. It knocked me off the pedestal everyone had me on. And I was ready, willing, and able, with conscious choice, to violate fundamental moral values, and that was a shocking discovery for me. And it was—it was a painful discovery to realize I was like everybody else."

At the peak of my own self-loss, I started to experience mental health struggles for the first time. It made me feel less connected to, and ashamed of, my Self. How could a therapist-in-training be having panic attacks or—when things were especially bad—dissociating? I remember walking to my therapist's office and being incredibly distressed because I couldn't feel my body, I couldn't sense the ground I was walking on. In this state, I felt like I no longer possessed myself; the self-disconnect manifested on a visceral level.

Facing ourselves and our humanity is the *only* way to identify our self-loss. During the Covid-19 pandemic, many of us experienced an identity crisis as a consequence of our lives being threatened, our daily routines being drastically altered, and our choices being narrowed. We could no longer go to our offices, jet to new locations, celebrate events, or hang out in bars. Many of us lost jobs and loved ones. Those of us whose sense of Self had been hijacked by our professional and social roles felt lost when we were no longer able to perform them.

The pandemic caused a mass awakening for us in terms of acknowledging and evaluating our self-relationship by stripping us of expectations, mindless routines, and distractions. I think we can all agree that being stuck at home in our own company had a merciless way of highlighting the degree to which our sense of Self was masked by external things or people. It made us realize the lack of alignment and resonance we had with our own lives—many of us, without realizing it, caught a first glimpse of our self-loss.

Rules and Modeled Behaviors

Camilla took out her phone right as our session started. She looked at me and said that she had something she would like to read out loud—a family text. I waited for her with anticipation, having no idea what the topic of today's session might be. She cleared her throat and began, "Family rule number one: All our children are expected to treat their body with modesty, refraining from all sexual activity. Family rule number two: Children are in no position to question or challenge decisions made by parents. Family rule number three: All siblings are expected to share with a parent any information that another sibling is hiding. Family rule number four: Family is, and should be, the number one priority for each and every member. Family rule number five: Tattoos and piercings are not allowed. Family rule number six: Caffeine, alcohol, and sugar are not to be consumed in moderation but rather abstained from entirely. Family rule number seven: Attending Sunday services is mandatory. Family rule number eight . . ."

I sat there, shocked. I was not expecting a list of rules. The client—who was in her mid-thirties, had a successful career as a lawyer, and lived on her own—proceeded to tell me that today's text was just an *updated* version of the "family rules" and that each member was expected to respond, acknowledging that they planned to honor the wishes of their father (the author of the text). Any violation was to be punished by "exclusion from family activities."

Her mother had been the first to respond, with approval.

Camilla didn't say much once she finished reading, but suddenly she began to sob. She was frustrated, unsure how to reconcile the demands of her family and her own, very separate, life. She felt pulled in different directions and she couldn't figure out how to hold the multiple seemingly contradictory beliefs that resonated with her. There was no way for her to please everyone, and that crushed her.

Camilla's experience illustrates the point that our understanding of who we are is always impacted by the rules and modeled behaviors we grew up with. Individuals who grew up in systems that allowed very little space for them to express—and consequently *be*—who they are often struggle with self-loss. If we are taught that we are not allowed to exist in a way that differs from what is expected (or risk rejection and abandonment), we will likely seek our sense of Self in approval.

Although very few people receive texts that explicitly state the family rules, almost everyone feels them implicitly. Which family rules have shaped the way you understand your Self? Which rules clash with how you experience your Self? And, most important, how has Self or authenticity been modeled to you (if at all)?

Many of us grew up with parents who struggled with their own sense of Self and exhibited behaviors that we are now unknowingly repeating. If we didn't have parents who modeled freedom, responsibility, choice, and authenticity, what are the chances that we will naturally know how to?

Our biological family is a "given," it is not something we can change. But it's up to *us* to seek embodiment and oneness with our Self—the antithesis of self-loss—by acknowledging the possibility of what we can become and what family cycles we want to break.

Self-Betrayal in Relationships

Rollo May, an American existential psychologist and author, wrote: "If you do not express your own original ideas, if you do not listen to your own being, you will have betrayed yourself." "Self-betrayal" is not a clinical diagnosis, but the term is often used within the mental health and self-help community to describe when one denies parts of one's Self (e.g., needs, thoughts, and feelings) for the sake of another person, job, relationship, etc. Basically, it's whenever we choose something, or someone, over our Self. It's when we shift our loyalty from us to something external. It's not about compromising on trivial matters such as which train to take or which restaurant to go to; it's when we take actions that compromise who we *are*.

> Existential analysis poses an important question: "What gets lost when I do things that are not me?"
>
> The answer: "*I* get lost. I lose myself. I become a stranger to myself."

Sometimes our self-betrayal takes an extreme form of willingness to do something that hurts us in order to please others, or in a misguided attempt to "keep" someone. Many of us are terrified to be alone, and we are willing to sacrifice whatever it takes to not face loneliness. Yet, in an effort to possess someone else, we lose possession of our Self. André Gide, a French writer and Nobel Prize winner, said: "The fear of finding oneself alone—that is what they suffer from—and so they don't find themselves at all."

Self-betrayal shifts our focus away from our Self, leading us to find our motivation outside of who we are. This transition is often gradual and not something we are aware of. Maybe it starts with a small action, such as saying *yes* when we want to say *no*, but it can quickly turn into responding to people and situations in the way we anticipate *they* want, rather than in alignment with what *we* need. Our actions determine who we become and, simultaneously, they speak to the current relationship we have with our Self (authentic or inauthentic).

I've had several clients tell me that a person in their life doesn't "deserve" their authenticity. My response is always the same: "*Who* do you think authenticity is for?" This question is often met with silence-filled contemplation or a cheeky (perhaps annoyed) smile.

Of course, authenticity helps us create healthy relationships with those around us, but it's also the foundation of a healthy relationship with our Self.

Authenticity is, above all else, *for us*. And yet, many of us believe it's for others. And since we believe it's for others, we are often willing to sacrifice it for others. In my private practice and research, I've observed that self-betrayal occurs most frequently in romantic relationships (although familial relationships are a close second). It can look like:

- Changing yourself to be who your partner wants you to be
- Denying problems in the relationship (even if they hurt you)
- Silencing your voice/intuition (because it threatens your relationship)
- Engaging in undesired intimacy (to please your partner)
- Accepting less than you deserve
- Compromising your beliefs and values
- Apologizing for things that are not your fault
- Not speaking up for your needs
- Crossing your own boundaries in order to make your partner happy
- Lying in order to keep the peace
- Making yourself small in order for others to feel better about themselves
- Sacrificing your autonomy

- Doing things that are disrespectful or demeaning toward your Self
- Hesitating to stand up for your Self
- Focusing on fulfilling the needs of others over your own
- Not valuing or investing in the relationship with who you are (because your time and energy is given to "them")

I see many clients who come to therapy because they want to make their relationship work. But whenever the reason for therapy seems to be solely centered around a relationship (or another person), what I get most curious about is the relationship the client has with themselves.

For years, I worked closely with one client, Naomi, an incredibly thoughtful, gentle, and hilarious millennial. She also struggled with feeling insecure, setting boundaries, and loving and knowing her Self. She was frightened of losing her partner, but, most important, she was terrified of being alone. No matter how difficult, draining, or unhealthy the relationship became, she never considered leaving. Naomi didn't recognize her own value enough to genuinely believe that she deserved better or that someone would be willing to offer it to her. Instead, she stayed with a partner who had multiple affairs he didn't bother to hide, stole her mom's prescription pills, impulsively spent their savings, disappeared for days at a time without telling her where he went, never introduced her to his friends, and seemed almost entirely disinterested in physical intimacy.

It took her years before she recognized that staying in the

relationship was self-betrayal. With time, she was able to acknowledge that no matter how hard she tried to be the "perfect" partner and "earn" his attention and love, he was simply incapable of giving it to her. Naomi gave too much and asked for nothing in return. And this is the thing about generosity: *Effort and loyalty without boundaries can become a form of self-betrayal.* Not only did she compromise who she was for the relationship; as a consequence, she eventually didn't know who she was at all. The unfortunate reality is that many of us are placed in situations in which we ultimately have to choose between two people—one being our Self.

Besides wanting to keep someone in our life, there are other reasons we may do things that don't align with us:[*]

- We lack self-awareness.
- We are seduced, coerced, forced, or pressured.
- We feel obligated (out of a sense of loyalty, morality, or belief structure).

Sometimes it's a combination of all of these reasons.

Jonah married his grad school girlfriend because she gave him an ultimatum on graduation day: get married or break up. According to him, getting married was a "cognitive" decision, not one founded in love (and, as we know, inner consent isn't merely cognitive!). When I asked why he decided to get married, he said it was his sense of responsibility and fear of loneliness that outweighed the way he felt about her and the

---

[*] This list was taken from a workshop taught by Längle.

relationship. I admired the fact that he took responsibility for his decision.

"But I would say I was a willing agent that contributed to my self-betrayal. As I look back, if I made different choices at different times and was more true to myself, I would have made different decisions, rather than making decisions out of concern and affection for [others]. I should have been tougher at the time, and we probably shouldn't have gotten married. And I felt obligated to marry her. And I felt my feelings were secondary to protecting her . . . I thought at the time it was a sensible decision. Because even though I didn't feel one hundred percent good about it, it was the right thing to do."*

Self-betrayal is a form of inauthenticity. It's important to ask ourselves the question: "How does it feel—or, what do I sense—when I do things that I can't really stand behind?" In other words, how does it feel when we agree to do something that does not align with us, or something that we feel forced to do out of a sense of "correctness" or high moral ground?

We often feel the following:†

- Controlled rather than in control (and subjected to a "foreign" power)
- Lack of presence in the current moment

---

* This quote is transcribed verbatim from interviews I conducted during my MA research.
† This list was taken from a workshop taught by Längle.

- Emptiness
- Loss of time
- Lack of connection with our Self during those acts

Whether it's attending a family event, working on the weekends, or laughing at offensive jokes—situations in which we know, deep down, we cannot give our inner consent will estrange us from our Self. What often hurts the most about self-betrayal is our *participation*. It's painful to face our own actions, and as much as we want to place the responsibility on others, it ultimately belongs to us.

A Desire to Be Lost

Finally, there is one other cause or reason for self-loss: *We WANT to be lost.* A relationship with the Self is grounding, fulfilling, and liberating, but it's also *hard*. Some people don't want to carry the burden of Self. They find comfort in self-deceit, ignorance, or performance. They don't want anything in their lives to change; and they don't want to have to change. People who find life absurd and inherently meaningless sometimes can't be bothered with trying to reap the benefits of freedom, choice, and responsibility—they've opted out for the satisfaction that comes with hedonism or the comfort that comes with the loss.

ROLE-PLAY: HOW WE PARTICIPATE IN OUR SELF-LOSS

I hadn't realized the role I played in my self-loss until I began therapy, right after my panic attack in California. Every time I walked into my therapist's office, my jaw relaxed and the tension in my shoulders released. I felt safe, a rare thing for someone who wasn't grounded in her Self. The second I sank into the couch, I'd begin to confess. More to my Self than to her. I would utter thoughts that felt too threatening or overwhelming to be expressed in solitude. It was the one hour a week that I allowed my Self to surrender, which at times felt a lot like losing control.

But surrendering is not about losing control. It's about relinquishing our *illusion* of control and responding to life's questions and demands with curiosity and openness. In order for us to face our loss, identify its cause, and explore the role we play in it, three prerequisites are needed:

1. **Self-awareness.** Self-awareness is our ability to *see* our Self and understand how we are operating in the world, usually through acts of introspection and reflection. Self-awareness requires constant observation of our emotions, thoughts, and behaviors in order to become conscious of how we are experiencing our lives, our relationships, and our Selves.

   Self-awareness allows us to encounter our own individuality and authenticity. It's important to note, though, that awareness is not limited to acknowledging the good; it involves facing our mistakes, shortcomings, and struggles. Irvin D. Yalom—a renowned American existential psychiatrist—states that "despair is the price one pays for self-awareness. Look deeply into life, and you'll always find despair." Why? Because existence always comes with despair, and awareness always brings this despair to light. This is why so many of us dwell in denial and willful ignorance—we want to avoid feeling misery and pain. And this is why so many of us remain unaware that we're lost, and blind to the role we play in our own predicament.

2. **Honesty.** Encountering ourselves is only possible if we are honest about what we observe and experience. We need to practice being honest about what and who we *see*. And we must learn to be honest not only *with* ourselves, but also *about* ourselves. Honesty requires us to practice facing the truth, even if it causes discomfort.

   We need to stop pretending that we are not hurt by the things that hurt us. We need to stop pretending that we don't want the things we want. We need to stop pretending that our actions don't have consequences. We need to stop pretending that we are not responsible for the life we live. We need to stop pretending that we don't have the freedom of choice (regardless of how large or small). We need to stop pretending, and we need to practice being honest.

3. **Safety.** "The real question is: How much truth can I stand?" Yalom poses an interesting point here. The weight of honesty can only be carried by *choice*. When we do not choose the truth, it can become crushing, consuming, or even destructive—it can become something we cannot bear. We must feel *safe* enough in order to "stand" or coexist with the truth.

   If we struggle with honesty, the point is not to break through our denial; rather it is to find ways to, first, enhance our sense of safety. When we don't have safety within our Self, we often feel the need to control everything and everyone in order to naturalize the perceived threats. I relied on my therapist to ground and protect me from my own painful thoughts. I needed her until I eventually had my Self; until I trusted my Self enough to not crumble upon facing my reality. It took me a while to learn the art of surrender, and I found it in the realization that the fine line between surrender and being out of control is *safety*.

This is not a reason—nor an excuse—to avoid the truth. Not facing our Self has equally painful consequences. So if avoidance isn't the answer, what is? *Patience*. In my clinical work, I notice that as time goes on, clients are willing to accept greater degrees of their truth. The level of their willingness correlates directly with the level of intimacy, safety, and trust they have with themselves.

Taylor was a client who manifested particularly unhealthy and harmful coping mechanisms. We spent months unpacking their life story, and although they were exhibiting clear signs of early childhood trauma, they never brought it up. It would have been easy to probe, but I chose not to. Eventually, after some time, Taylor confirmed my suspicion by sharing a traumatic childhood experience, one that they were still having a hard time admitting happened. My job was to never push the truth on them before they could bear it. My job was to help them grow in self-trust and inner safety so they could *choose* to face it. Ultimately, *we* are the only ones who can decide how much we can handle. We have to find our own pace.

Safety and trust cannot be disentangled, because one does

not exist without the other. There are many life experiences that may challenge our *fundamental trust*. "Fundamental trust" is an existential analysis term that refers to the ground of our very Being; what I perceive to be the support we cannot live without. The foundation can help us trust in our ability to exist, fully and authentically, in the world. No matter what we are going through—what we have done or what has been done to us—we are all faced with this question:

What grounds my trust? Or, in other words: *What is the basis of my trust?*

There are three common answers:

1. Myself and my own life
2. Somebody or something
3. God or some larger, encompassing organizing principle

Ultimately, the ability to ground our trust creates the internal sense of safety that's necessary for us to practice awareness and honesty. Our fundamental trust allows us to acknowledge the role we've played in our self-loss. There are three types of roles we can play:

1. **A victim:** someone who experiences self-loss as a consequence of events occurring outside of their control (e.g., trauma) that have disrupted their sense of Self. It's important to note that I don't believe we can be victims of self-loss in the long-term (see #3), because that would mean

there are contexts that alleviate us of our responsibility permanently.

2. **An agent:** someone whose own decisions have led to the experience of self-loss (e.g., self-betrayal).

3. **Both (victim and agent):** an individual who experienced events out of their control that disrupted their sense of Self, but who has also made decisions that have perpetuated self-loss.

Arguably, most of us fall into the third category.

This is why, in my first session with every client, I always start with the same activity, an exercise that helps me gain insight into the way the person sees and experiences their Self (or how they don't). It's called *Lifeline,** and how it works is simple. I ask the client to tell me any and all significant events that have happened to them, from the moment they were born until now (I said it was simple, not easy!). The experiences don't have to be "objectively" significant, they should just be ones that stand out to *them*. I've heard it all—from being sent to bed hungry to fun memories of swimming with Dad—and the wonderful thing is that it doesn't matter what the event was. What matters is the meaning the client has attributed to it; the recognition that these events have *shaped* who they are.

Want to try it? Take out a piece of paper and draw a long horizontal line across it. Where the line begins, write "zero," and where the line ends, write your current age. Then, for

---

* I learned this cognitive behavioral therapy activity from my practicum supervisor my very first week seeing clients. Since then, I've continued to alter it to make it my own and to resonate with my individual clients.

every event, draw a vertical line (either up or down, depending on whether it was positive or negative) and write the year, one word that describes the event, and one word that summarizes the impact or feeling. This is a great exercise to give your Self space to reflect on your existence, your patterns, your relationships, your resilience, your wounds, your formative moments. See what happens. See if you gain a deeper understanding of who you are, even if you are feeling a bit lost right now. Remember that you may not understand your Self, because you may not understand all the circumstances that led you to who you are now. Take a moment to reflect on all the moments—big and small—that led you to be sitting where you are *right now*.

LIFELINE

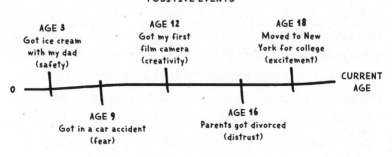

POSITIVE EVENTS

AGE 3
Got ice cream with my dad (safety)

AGE 12
Got my first film camera (creativity)

AGE 18
Moved to New York for college (excitement)

0   CURRENT AGE

AGE 9
Got in a car accident (fear)

AGE 16
Parents got divorced (distrust)

NEGATIVE EVENTS

WE MUST BE THE PROTAGONISTS OF OUR LIVES

Please indulge me, once again, as I illustrate an important point through a scene from a popular rom-com, this time *The Holiday*, starring Kate Winslet and Cameron Diaz. A scene in which Iris (one of the main characters, struggling with unrequited love, played by Winslet) is talking to her new friend Arthur Abbott (a famous screenwriter who is about ninety years old) about her life. He listens to her carefully, and then replies:

> ARTHUR: Iris, in the movies we have leading ladies, and we have the best friend. You, I can tell, are a leading lady, but for some reason, you're behaving like the best friend.
>
> IRIS: You're so right. You're supposed to be the leading lady of your own life, for god's sake! Arthur, I've been going to a therapist for three years, and she's never explained anything to me that well. That was brilliant. Brutal, but brilliant.

Do you know who the main character of *your* life is?

Imagine watching a movie *without* a main character. How confusing would it be to follow the plotline or truly understand the narrative, context, or perspective of the film? Likewise, in life, we cease to understand what our actions, decisions, and emotions truly mean if we are not connected to our Self; if we are not looking at our one, particular life as a meaningful and true movie in which we are starring.

Being the protagonist of your own life—your own story—is not about being self-centered; it's about being self-aware and self-attuned. And it is only through our *actions* that we transform self-awareness into self-attunement.

A year after I started seeing my therapist, I remember sitting on a stoop, journal in hand, crying with frustration that I didn't know what was wrong with me or why I hadn't "healed" yet. I'd done all the things that I thought I was meant to do. I'd left my unhappy marriage, I'd started therapy, I journaled and traveled. I made all the changes I could think of, so why was I still hurting? Why was I still lost?

At that time in my life, I felt rushed to purge *all* my pain, to heal everything, *right away*. I was "correcting" all the major mistakes I'd made—but I was still not fully encountering my Self. The thing I can see now is that I wanted to recognize my essence, but I wanted to do it without coming too close to it (which, I should note, is an impossible line to walk). I was ready for the "work" to be over already, but it was just beginning (and, little did I know, it would never end).

Even after a year of intensive therapy and intentional life changes, I couldn't give wholehearted inner consent to my life. It took many more years before that would come. *And still*, the time I've spent rebuilding a relationship with my Self was not lost. I need you to know that if you feel like you're stumbling in the dark, this time is *still* profoundly valuable, it's still important—it is not a waste. *Learning* to live as my Self was the lesson and the goal itself.

Maybe you've tried to cultivate your sense of Self by listening to or appeasing others. Maybe you used to know who you were but have lost sight of who that is along the way. Maybe you've experienced something that left you feeling like a different version of your Self. Maybe life never gave you the space to figure out who you are—or maybe you've never cared to find out. Regardless of why you are experiencing the consequences of self-loss, you *can* do something about it.

There is something empowering about knowing that we've

shaped previous versions of ourselves (even if they do not serve us). Why? Because that means we have the power to shape who we want to become.

Life is certainly not about *only* focusing on your Self, but I want you to know that it's okay to think about your Self, prioritize your Self, and even love your Self. I also want—need—you to know that there is no other way to actually exist.

Hard Truth

If you're not honest about the story that got you here, you'll never change the narrative.

Gentle Reminder

Be the leading character in your own life.

CHAPTER 5

How Does Society Perpetuate Self-Loss?

Sam was in her late thirties when she first came to see me. She was in a great deal of pain, but it would have been hard for anyone to tell (although the fact that she was in therapy tipped me off). During our first couple of sessions, she presented as an "ideal" client—always showing up on time, greeting me with enthusiasm and asking about my day, doing her "homework," and articulating all her points eloquently and clearly. She was wonderful—and I quickly began to worry that it was performative. I didn't discount her efforts as ungenuine, but I did worry that she felt she had to do or *be* certain things in order to fulfill expectations or emulate a "good" client.

At the start of our work together, I noticed that Sam would often apologize whenever she would cry or swear—expressing worry that this was not how she "should" be behaving. I soon became curious about the expectations and "rules" that appeared to be guiding her life, her interactions, and, most important, her sense of Self.

One of the many wonders of a therapeutic relationship is that it provides a unique space for the client to mimic or mirror their experience with others—often unconsciously. This process allows the therapist to slowly understand how the client shows up, engages with others, and experiences their own inner world. As for me and Sam, I immediately struggled to shake the feeling that she was coming to therapy with a set "script"—one she used with everyone in her life. While I couldn't be sure, I knew one thing: I wasn't really *seeing* Sam. Rather, I was observing who she thought she had to be. As we began to unpack her upbringing, we slowly unearthed strict cultural and religious frameworks. Her adoptive parents had emphasized the importance of obedience and selflessness above all else. These were the two principles that had guided her life, and arguably ruined it. Her entire script boiled down to one demand, to one specific, and unfortunately common, imposition: *Be a "good girl."*

For her, this meant that she gained her value by being helpful, needed, or wanted by others. She was asked to know her worth, but to stay silent when her boundaries were crossed. She was taught that she needed to smile, and to conceal her wounds, feelings, and power. She was expected to always give more than she took. She embodied what *others* needed her to be. She was asked to be attractive but innocent; sexy but not sexual. She learned about pleasure as something she offered, not as something she received. She was expected to achieve a lot, but to never talk about it (for pride is unseemly!). She was always put-together—her body following the desired trends, shapes, and weight of the times. She was asked to be confident, but only to the degree to which it wouldn't threaten others. She was polite, articulate, and educated, but was expected to often refrain from speaking her mind. She didn't talk back or confront others, and, most important, as a good girl, she did as she was told.

Even in her thirties, Sam—who was married and had three kids—was still abiding by these rules. That's because there is no expiration date for conformity; there is no set age at which society sets us free. Violations in the form of peer pressure, shaming, and expectations persist throughout our life, morphing in shape to reflect life's different stages.

For Sam, successfully meeting expectations set by society gave her a sense of accomplishment and fleeting moments of acceptance. It was not until she understood the inauthenticity in which she was steeped that she realized the responsibility, choices, and power she had unknowingly relinquished.

One day, after roughly a year of working together, she began the session by bursting into the room and exclaiming, "You are going to be so proud of me!" The truth was, I was already proud of her on a weekly basis, but I was still curious about what she was going to say. (Plus, "good girls" don't often offer self-compliments, so I was excited about where this was going.) "I set my very first boundary—*ever*. I am thirty-nine years old, and I have never set a boundary until today!"

She was right; I couldn't have been more proud of her.

Sam had been asked by her boss to take on a responsibility that was not hers, and to attend meetings after her designated hours (which, historically, she had never been compensated for). In the past, she unflinchingly did as asked, but on this particular day she said, "I have reached my maximum work-load and I will not be available for the seven P.M. meeting." And to her surprise, the world didn't end.

From that moment on, she began to question what it meant to be "good." Not only what her family deemed good but what society labeled as such. She questioned why she grew up being rewarded for thoughtless conformity (and subservience to the patriarchy). *Who* exactly had chosen who she became? Where was her freedom (did she really lose it, or had she just failed to use it)? How did she manage to melt into the *"they"* of society without being aware of it?

Sam is certainly not alone. Heidegger wrote about this phenomenon of being lost in the "they" of society. If we pay close enough attention, we will notice how brands, institutions, families, etc., often try to "relieve" us of our burden of making choices in our everyday lives. At some point, we may even find ourselves uncertain about who actually made our decisions. *How did we get here? Is this what we want? Is this who we are?* It's easy to get swept up by society, surrendering agency and falling more deeply into inauthenticity (or worse yet, self-loss). According to Heidegger: "This process can be reversed. . . . This must be accomplished by making up for not choosing."

In other words, in our society, we no longer feel the responsibility to choose who we become. It's been "decided" for us. We are shaped by society because of our passivity. Society has given us *permission* to be inauthentic—which renders us even more lost. We can *be* our Selves once we recognize the difference between "I" and "they" and become active participants in creating who we are.

Most of us would hope that others—"they"—would have our backs, but instead we're left feeling discouraged and betrayed by the people around us. Now we are desperately trying to unlearn the many lessons about who they told us to be. And here is the hard truth we can't ignore: We are all a part of the "they" of society. We have all acted as a "they" to someone. Our actions not only shape us, they can also have real impact on those around us. We have all done, taught, or modeled things to others that they will have to unlearn or heal from.

As a society, we are given people and trends to aspire to—yet often these things do not align with us. We accept all of it, though, because we want to belong or, sometimes, because we can't be bothered to figure out what *does* align (and as a result, we end up perpetuating the problem for future generations). The hardest part for Sam was *recognizing* that her "inner circles"—as well as society at large—had participated in, and benefited from, her self-loss. And by being who they needed her to be, she gave them an out from responsibility for their actions (she always pretended things were great); she helped them protect their own narratives about what kind of parents her mother and father were (she never constructed a narrative herself); and they used her talents, selflessness, and skills to better their own lives (she was taught that making their lives easier should be one of her main priorities).

She was someone they relied on, but didn't bother to know.

And Sam is not alone. Many of us carry our own versions of being "good" rather than being *us*. We are encouraged to be a good girl, a good neighbor, a good believer, a good employee, a good student, a good son/daughter/mother/father, etc. Dangerously, we've also implicitly begun attributing moral values to labels. Meaning that when we fail, refuse to conform, or to live up to the many expectations of us, we are considered "bad." When we do obey and perform, we are considered "good." The system was not created for authenticity, and the individuals who manage to embody it are often victims of moral criticism and societal resistance, if not condemnation. And this begins at a young age. Most of us have been told we were "wrong" or needed to "change" as children—before we even had the chance to truly create who we are. We were categorized as "bad" for exploring, expressing, and coloring outside the lines. Early on, we were presented with a choice between conformity or rejection.

Don't get me wrong, the need to be accepted is normal, and not one we should villainize. But choosing who we seek and receive acceptance from is where the magic and our freedom lie.

PREREQUISITES TO HAVING A SENSE OF SELF

Rollo May said, "Every human being must have a point at which he stands against the culture, where he says, this is me, and the damned world can go to hell."

This is a tempting, rousing mindset, but it's unrealistic.

Although we can't surrender to the inauthenticity encouraged by societal structures, we can't fully ignore it either.

In existential analysis, we see the Self in terms of two poles ("mirrors")—inside and outside—which are important for our view of Self. The *inside pole* reflects to us how we experience our Self *and* evaluates how accurately the "outside" reflection agrees with our own evaluation. The *outside pole* shows us what of our Self is being reflected back to us through things such as relationships, outcomes, and successes. Then, we are asked to once again reflect on who we are, and whether the outside reflection agrees with our own new understanding. It's a circle, a cycle. Without the outer pole, we can become self-satisfied, smug, or have narcissistic tendencies. Without the inner pole, we can become *lost*. Plainly, as Längle once said in class, "there is no Self without the *other*." We all need a mirror in order to see who we are. But what happens when the mirror is warped?

Imagine that you are getting ready for an important event. You leave the house feeling comfortable and confident— secretly looking forward to what others will say, or think, when they see you. Once you arrive, you immediately begin to notice that no one is making eye contact with you. They seem to pass you quickly, awkwardly glancing at you, and sometimes even chuckling. You look down but everything seems to be fitting well. Several minutes later a child runs up to you and innocently asks, "Why are you dressed like that? It's silly." Horrified, you run to the bathroom and look in the full-length mirror—but all you see is *you*. You cannot see what others seem to see. You muster the courage to ask the person who is standing near you, clearly judging you, to describe what you're wearing. They look you up and down and, with a look of disdain, say, "A clown suit."

What happens when we act authentically and it's not accepted? What happens when the way we see our Self is not the way others see us? Such incongruence shakes our understanding of who we are. It makes us question what we "see." And in the worst-case scenarios, it makes us act in a way that corresponds with how others see us. *You see a clown, I'll be a clown*. The search and creation of Self becomes more difficult if others keep demanding, rewarding, and reflecting inauthentic versions of us. What if our mentors, role models, or community have preconceived notions of who we should be?

In different areas of our lives, these demands may sound something like:

- **Family system:** "Be yourself, but only as long as you don't diverge from family norms; and keep following family rules."
- **Institutions:** "Be yourself and 'think outside the box,' but don't question the system."
- **Brands:** "Be yourself, but only in this very specific way (which you can achieve by buying these products or adopting these ideas)."
- **Friends:** "Be yourself, but only as long as you're the same as the rest of us."
- **Community:** "Be yourself, but only as long as it doesn't upset or challenge us."

But the danger of self-loss does not simply lie in the fact that we may be totally ignorant of who we are. Heidegger said that "faulty interpretations, misunderstandings, put much more stubborn obstacles in the way of authentic cognition than a total ignorance."

In our daily lives, there is ample opportunity for us to misunderstand or misinterpret our Self. We humans have this impressive and perplexing capacity to alter, mask, and shape-shift in order to satisfy family structures, communities, relationships, and whatever other needs or demands may be present in a given context. Due to our ability, and often willingness, to edit ourselves, we can create a great deal of inner confusion. When our actions are incongruent with the way we perceive our Self, or with what we believe to be right or wrong, we are left questioning who we are.

In order to understand our profound distinctiveness, relevance, and meaning—and embody our authentic Self—there are three prerequisites that we need: *attention, appreciation, and justice,* which I will discuss in detail in the next few pages. Often, society offers these things in a way that reinforces who *it* wants us to be, rather than who *we* are. Unfortunately, our communities are not always inclusive or accepting of everyone; therefore, it's not safe for everyone to *be* who they are. Society does offer attention, appreciation, and justice, but not to all, and not equally.

So, what can we do to be our Self within such a dysfunctional structure?

First, we must find a clear mirror within society—people who are *willing* to get to know us enough to reflect back accurately and give us permission to be our Self. People who are willing to *see* us. And it's on us to select *who* we want to impact us (because inevitably someone, or something, will—for better or for worse).

Next, we need to be willing to accept attention, appreciation, and justice from others *and* offer it to ourselves. This is what makes the process difficult; we must receive these things internally *and* externally. The most important relationship you will ever have is with your Self, but this relationship is not independent of others. It's our responsibility to be intentional about who we surround ourselves with. In doing so, we get to decide *whose* attention, appreciation, and justice we want, and what to do with it. This is about so much more than our preferences; it's about *shaping our very existence.* Choosing who you surround yourself with, to a degree, is choosing who you become.

Let's go through these prerequisites to having a sense of Self:

Attention

We all have the need to be *seen.* Attention—or having someone recognize and validate that we, in fact, exist—is critical to our existence. If we've been deprived of genuine attention, if we've been neglected, we may settle for merely being *noticed.* The difference between being noticed and being offered attention is similar to that between *looking* and *seeing.* We can look at something without registering it or understanding it, while seeing entails looking with intention; seeing entails *understanding. True* attention is about being acknowledged, *known,* and *recognized* for who we really are, by people who know us. It's about them seeing us in a way that aligns with how we see our Self (flaws, strengths, experiences, and all). In other words, we only experience genuine attention when the person is attuned to who we are, truly—when their understanding of us reflects the way we understand our Self. (Tip*: If you are struggling to discern genuine attention from being noticed, instead of asking yourself, "Are they paying attention to me?" try asking, "Are they attuned to who I am? Do I feel like they know me?"*)

"Attention seekers"—usually—are not individuals with in-

flated egos but rather people with a precarious sense of Self—
they are looking for others to define or validate their Self.
Again, many of us didn't grow up having our emotions, needs,
desires, or opinions heard. This leads to a scarcity mindset,
which leads us to compete for attention. Our shared wound
has created a culture that forces us to showcase our differences, pain, and vulnerabilities in an effort to be "interesting"
enough for people to notice us among all the clutter.

How devastating is it for us to live in a world such as this,
where value is not placed on being our Self but on our ability
to grab and keep another's attention? And then! When we do
eventually get noticed—when the algorithms are in our fa-
vor—by a stranger, or that random friend we went to high
school with, or that person we met at the bar—the connection
is as shallow as the fleeting satisfaction that comes with it. It's
a relentless cycle of disappointment.

Ultimately, the *only* way we can feel understood by others
is if we understand our Self. The onus is on us, and—as I'll
keep saying—it's not always easy (in fact, it's not *often* easy).
Being busy has become an admirable way to avoid our Self.
Being our Self insists that we cut through the noise, demands, and expectations so that we can be still and present. It
means overcoming the constant temptation to escape, ignore,
or numb ourselves to experience. *True self-attention requires
self-perception*. It asks us to be aware and observant, so that
ultimately we may experience who we are, fully.

We want others to see us the way we see our Self. But that's
only possible if *we* know what we look like. If we don't, we
will offer an incongruent image that others will not be able to
comprehend. In return, they will reflect a fragmented or pro-

jected image back to us. But most of us will take anything we can get, because *an individual who desperately seeks attention is just a human with an unmet need to be seen.*

Social media, for example, promises to fulfill this important human need to be seen and often makes us feel like it does, but the feeling is temporary. What social media actually offers is endless opportunity to be *noticed*. It gives attention in the form of praise and validation for our looks, output, or entertainment value—generally, by acquaintances or complete strangers. They notice you exist, but they don't acknowledge who you really are (to be fair, it would be difficult for them to do so in that kind of context). These contexts and platforms will begin to shape who we become by merely reinforcing certain aspects of ourselves while ignoring others. And eventually we will begin to do the same, further distorting our sense of Self.

Right before I started my Instagram account, I had a consultation session with a fellow therapist who was further along in her social media journey. The advice she gave me was to find my voice and lean into it. It was interesting—and felt odd—to think about what that meant. *What is my voice?* The more I attempted to curate it perfectly, the more confused I became.

Eventually I just stopped asking, "What should Sara the 'therapist' be like?" and began to ask, "What describes this moment and/or this phenomenon in a way that *I* understand?" I gave people information as I saw and understood it, and unknowingly, I gave them glimpses of my true Self. It stopped being about some preconceived notion of Self that I was attempting to capture for the sake of others. It stopped being about trying to be the person I imagined followers were look-ing for. It became about *alignment*.

In short, I stopped asking, "How will people experience me?" and started asking, "How do *I* experience my Self?"

———

I remember one particularly difficult session with a client. Erin sat in front of me, distraught, exploring an old wound that was causing her to unravel. It was a wound we had ad-dressed several times, but this time she was finally willing to really sit with it. Her sobs were echoing her feelings of being unseen. With pain-stricken words, she described how she was not given attention from her family, friends, former partners, or, even now, from strangers at a bar. I was puzzled. *Why were others not seeing what she saw? Or, what I saw?*

We'd already been working together for several months at this point, and although I deeply felt her pain, I noticed a pat-tern of her concealing her feelings, opinions, and body from others. I got the sense that she was not really showing her Self. Our conversation went something like this:

ERIN: I feel invisible [*quietly sobbing*], no one sees me. No one ever has.

ME: I'm sorry, it sounds incredibly painful.

ERIN: [*nods and wipes her tears*]

ME: [*sits in silence for a few seconds*] I can't help but won-der, do you *want* to be seen?

ERIN: [*a flicker of shock and a long pause*] Yes . . . Well, I mean, *everyone* wants to be seen.

ME: [*nods*]

ERIN: [*stares into space, then begins to cry again*] Maybe I
    don't. No, no I don't.
ME: What do you think they will see? Or, what are you
    scared they will see?
ERIN: They will see nothing. That I am nothing.
ME: Hm. And you? What do you see?
ERIN: Nothing.

Ah, and there it is. The fear that prevents us from showing
up. **We cannot expect attention without attendance.** We must
show ourself—our true Self—in order to be seen. If we are
scared that there is "nothing" within us, we may desperately
try to avoid having that reflected back to us. But the truth is, if
we see "nothing," then we are not looking at our Self. Instead,
we're probably blind to the Self—a thick veil of pain, denial,
and failure prompting us to believe we're hollow.

We talk about our need to be seen, yet we must also acknowledge the difficulty. There is a *vulnerability* to being seen,
a risk of being rejected—it's scary! And let's face it, many of
us would rather be rejected for who we are *not* than for who
we are.

How do you feel about being seen for who you really are?
Here are some questions to reflect on:

- Do you feel like you have to compete for attention? If
  yes, with whom?
- Can you sense the difference between being seen and
  being noticed?
- Are you scared to be seen? Why or why not?
- What do people tend to notice about you?

- When you look at your Self, what do you see?
- What do you want to show people?
- Which part of you gets the most attention?
- Which part of you do you try to hide?
- Who gives you the most true attention?

Appreciation

Appreciation is not the same as attention. We all (probably) know that being acknowledged—getting attention—isn't the same thing as being *valued*. Appreciation is the step *beyond* mere acknowledgment. Once we are seen (truly seen), our inherent value also needs to be recognized. This is not the same as being offered spontaneous flattery or an enthusiastic thank-you. It's not a passive recognition of one's quality, contribution, or success. Rather, it's an active position that stems from attunement and *knowing* someone's worth. In existential analysis, we describe appreciation as standing up for someone's positive attributes—it's an *action* founded in conviction.

Unfortunately, we are often appreciated for what we can *do* for others, and rarely for who we are. Even more specifically, in our fast-paced society, we are often appreciated for our "usefulness" rather than our humanity. This type of appreciation puts us at risk for morphing into someone we are not. It can shift our understanding of Self to be other-focused, rather than self-focused—we begin to identify our sense of Self in comparison *to* others, *for* others, and as directed *by* others. We are more likely to allow others to *tell* us who we should be if we believe that we will be rewarded—appreciated—for embodying that role or persona.

Yet, what people—society—expect and ask of us is constantly changing. Thirty years ago, by age twenty-five, we "should" have been married, had a house with a white picket fence, a stable income, two kids (a boy and a girl), and a pet of some kind (preferably a golden retriever). Monogamy used to be the only acceptable relationship structure; now it can feel like it's not even a preferred one. Instead, many of us are told we "should" want to explore relationships without any set structure, work remotely, travel the world, have a social media presence, invest in cryptocurrency, do a job that is motivated by passion not income, and preferably work less than full-time. In our current culture, appreciation is often received for being unconventional, popular, and financially successful.

We all want to be appreciated, so we do what is expected, allowing arbitrary standards to define us. Just like body standards, our lifestyle trends are dictated and co-created by the *Other*. Although we can't escape the expectations, we can *choose* not to fulfill them. We can choose to seek appreciation for who we are, rather than for the boxes we have ticked off.

It's interesting that the current social narrative shames people for being too self-focused, but in reality, most people think of themselves primarily within the context of how *others* see them. In my opinion, most of us are not self-focused *enough*, not truly. We struggle to genuinely appreciate our Self because we struggle to acknowledge and accept who we are. Carl Jung said that "the most terrifying thing is to accept oneself completely." That's because it means not hiding or denying any aspect of our Self. And yet, instead of learning the art of self-acceptance, we are being taught how to earn or buy our acceptance from others. We are encouraged to "fix" or cover up our "shortcomings," rather than to practice honesty and vulnerability.

But I want to be clear: *It's not about ceasing to seek external validation; it's about seeking internal validation ABOVE external validation.* If we shift according to the appreciation of others, we will allow their opinions and feelings to lead us to inauthenticity or even self-loss—time and time again.

In order to begin to differentiate internal and external opinions, it's important to note the societal demands and "suggestions" we've internalized. Here are some questions to ask yourself:

- Who do I think I "should" be?
- What have I been taught about gender and sexuality?
- What do I believe my body should look like? Why?
- What do I believe should be my role in society?
- What have I been praised or punished for?
- What have I been taught to want?
- What have I been taught to fear?
- How do I define success?

What is *your* narrative about appreciation? Here are some more reflection questions to help you identify it.

- Who in my life appreciates me?
- From where do I derive my value?
- Do I appreciate my Self?
- What qualities do I love about who I am?
- What qualities make it difficult to appreciate my Self?

Justice

To be our Selves—to embrace our humanity—we need to be seen, appreciated, and *treated* as such. Justice is about being in alignment with one's Self, taking one's Self seriously, and being treated fairly by our Self and others. Unfairness or injustice within society is something we are starting to talk about more, but what we often overlook is how frequently we treat ourselves unfairly. Why can't we show ourselves the same kindness or offer forgiveness that we readily give others? Why do we put ourselves last, not meeting our own needs while ensuring everyone else's are met? Why do we have expectations for ourselves that are impossible? Why do we allow everyone else to be human but not our Selves?

Maybe you haven't been treated justly because of your nationality, the color of your skin, the beliefs you hold, that disgraced "divorced" status, the number on your scale, the amount of money in your bank account, or your gender or sexuality. Society has found endless ways to "justify" injustice. The illusive "they" evaluate and determine our worth and treat us accordingly. There is a famous quote attributed to Kierkegaard: "What labels me, negates me." When we label, we are forced to reduce. Once we are reduced to certain qualities, we are in danger of not being offered attention, appreciation, or justice.

For most of us, injustice was modeled or taught. Our caregivers may have emphasized or even romanticized self-sacrifice, instilling a sense of righteousness in being treated unfairly. As a Serbian woman, I was taught that I am "below" any male, and that my thoughts and feelings matter less than those of my elders.

For others, injustice was circumstantial. It wasn't fair for me, as a child, to not have enough food or to spend months in bomb shelters. It wasn't fair for me to have feared for my own survival and the survival of my parents. It wasn't fair that my Christmas gift when I was eight was a pen while other children got video games, chocolates, dolls, and whatever else they asked for.

Sometimes we are part of the injustice others are feeling, and we must work to acknowledge that we can *all* be part of the "they" of society. Perhaps we were raised with a sense of entitlement and privilege that oppresses others. Maybe we were taught (implicitly or explicitly) that because of our nationality, skin color, religious affiliation, relationship status, body shape, earning potential, gender, or sexuality, we are somehow entitled to be treated better than others. Perhaps our privilege has made us believe that the world owes us, that we deserve things even if others must suffer for us to get it. We may feel entitled to perpetuate injustice, because we believe that justice is only for us.

All the "isms" throughout history—racism, sexism, classism, etc.—have made collective justice difficult, if not impossible. We have mistreated whole groups of people, refusing to offer them attention, appreciation, or justice. We have not bothered to reflect to them their worth, and yet, when we treat others without human dignity, it only takes away our own.

WHEN OTHERS PUSH BACK, PUSH FORWARD

The act of living and creating our Self is inherently rewarding and fulfilling. *And,* in the same breath, such bravery—or, perhaps audacity—is often met with *resistance, isolation,* and *grief.* Every decision, even an authentic one, has a cost. This is why I want to normalize the price that comes with *being* your Self. In general, there are three types of drawbacks.

Drawback #1: Resistance

It's normal for all human beings to push back against anything unfamiliar, threatening, or that we perceive as potentially less beneficial. We gravitate toward comfort, predictability, and survival. Resistance from others is often not malicious or manipulative*—it's instinctual. Carl R. Rogers—an American psychologist and founder of the humanistic approach[†]—talks about fear as the root of resistance:

> If I let myself really understand another person, I might have to change by that understanding. And we all fear change. So as I say, it is not an easy thing to permit oneself to understand an individual, to enter thoroughly and completely and empathetically into his frame of reference.

We need to acknowledge that authenticity can be triggering for those around us. Our authenticity may highlight someone else's inauthenticity, or it may ask them to change the way they behave toward us. People may resist our sense of Self in

* I know we all love to focus on the "narcissists" of the world, but let's just assume that I am writing this for individuals who are not abusive or struggling with a personality disorder.

† Very simply, humanistic psychology is a perspective that humans, as individuals, are whole and unique. It emphasizes the personal worth of a person. Humanistic psychology holds the assumption that people have free will and are motivated to achieve self-actualization.

an effort to preserve the homeostasis of the relationship and avoid having to experience change themselves. Our self-awareness and embodiment will often come with new boundaries, lower levels of tolerance for mistreatment (aka we will stop putting up with shit), and higher standards (while maintaining realistic expectations). We are changing the nature of the relationship, the steps of the dance. If people want to continue dancing with us, they must learn the new choreography. Some will be unwilling, while others will step on our toes or awkwardly stumble at first.

So, don't hold back just because of this pushback. Let's refrain from assuming that those who, at first, show signs of resistance want us to remain inauthentic, or that they will never accept us. When we approach our Self with hesitation, we signal to others that there is still space for negotiation—when there isn't. Even a good change almost always involves loss and discomfort—so we must allow others time to grieve the previous version of us and the relationship dynamic we once had.

But, if resistance from those around us persists, it may be time to let go of a particular relationship. Because the truth is: *Chronic resistance is a form of rejection.*

Here are some common signs that you are facing resistance from another person:

- They keep reminding you of your past.
- They say, "You've changed," and don't mean it as a compliment.
- They challenge or violate your new boundaries.

- They keep using labels/adjectives that no longer apply to you.
- They make you feel guilty for taking care of yourself.
- They belittle or dismiss your growth.
- They call your sense of Self a "phase."
- They don't seem to understand you (no matter how hard you try to explain).
- They try to convince you of who you "really" are.
- They make condescending comments, mocking your truth.
- They threaten to end the relationship.

If we have a history of caving in, people will often resist us trying to enforce our true self. Others are likely to only push as far as they think they can—and usually, only as far as we've previously let them. I remember one of my clients being visibly distressed—flushed, teary-eyed, breathing heavily, and fidgeting with her hairband—as she spoke about the fact that she was meeting up with her ex-boyfriend right after our session. She'd wanted to set some boundaries with him for a while now, but was struggling to build up the courage. He hadn't responded well to her attempts during the relationship, and she expected the same reaction. The next session, she reported that despite the fact that she had spoken with tears streaming down her face, and with shaky, disjointed, and breathless words, she had finally stood up to her ex. To her surprise (but not mine), he quickly backed off. Sometimes the only reason people continually disrespect our boundaries is because we personally waver on them, failing to make them known.

This won't be the case in every situation, but it will be in more than we think. Many of us haven't given others the chance to grapple with our autonomy. We may fear that they will resist or reject us, but part of being brave is giving people (who deserve it) an opportunity to prove us wrong.

Lastly—and I know this may be difficult to hear—we are not simply *entitled* to be understood. We must be active participants; in order to be seen, we must *show* ourselves. Daring to show up as our authentic, unabashed Self means having to endure the discomfort of vulnerability and face the risk of rejection (if the situation is safe enough; if the person *deserves* to see our vulnerability). Never assume that other people will just "know," and that they will seamlessly change how they act. Some people may ask us to explain ourselves—and yes, not everyone is deserving of receiving an explanation, but some are. We only need to explain ourselves to the degree to which it will honor a specific relationship (the degree of intimacy and safety will dictate the level of disclosure). When we sense resistance, we must fight the instinct to ignore it. If the relationship is to survive, it's important to work to navigate the transition, together. Offer patience and compassion because it is not easy for them, just like it's not easy for us. We are in it together—*or not*.

It's also important to remember that this journey is not *for* others, and it's not something we can do *with* others. If we try to go about it that way, there is a high chance that our change will no longer align with us, or we will offload some of our responsibility onto someone to whom it doesn't belong—neither is helpful. It's inherently *for* you and *about* you. Try to not get upset if people do not want to accept who you have become. Again, we are not entitled to people accepting us, and oftentimes it's a big ask, given that most of us struggle to accept our Selves.

Drawback #2: Isolation

Seeking, creating, and embodying who we are is, obviously and unfortunately, not work we can outsource. Regardless of our familial and social support systems, there is something inherently isolating about the experience. The most someone else can do is guide, encourage, and witness our journey— reflect back to us how far we've come and what they *see*. But unless they are on a similar path themselves (and many aren't), they may not recognize or resonate with ours.

This process of separation is not always fully deliberate or blatant. It can come as a subtle feeling that we're in a different phase in life than those around us, that we are lacking things to talk about with people, or that our worldview has diverged from those of our family or friends. It can look like declining an invitation, ceasing to like people's Instagram pictures, or, eventually, not hanging out at all. When you bump into each other on the street you'll agree to "catch up sometime soon," but you both know that the sentiment is pleasantry rather than intention. Honestly, at first it can feel a little lonely—sad, even.

As we become more discerning about who we let in, we may begin growing apart from people who were once a big part of our lives. Our friends or family may complain that they no longer "understand" us, and they may keep reminding us of who we used to be. This may not be a sign of resistance; they may be telling us the truth—they simply *don't* understand who we are at this very moment.

For roughly five years following my life-changing panic attack, I remember feeling misunderstood, unacknowledged, and unappreciated. I hated it; I felt utterly alone. My decisions didn't make sense to people and instead of being curious about them, they judged. They judged me for getting a divorce, for selling all my things and traveling, for starting to date someone new (among many other new life choices I made). Pretty harshly, too. It hurt. It was only those who *wanted* to understand me that eventually did. And I learned the hard way that I would only be seen by those who *wanted* to see.

This is why I constantly validate the isolation that my clients feel when people are unwilling or unable to relate to the transformational process they are experiencing. It's hard for someone to fight for their freedom and existence while others won't even acknowledge the war. Don't be afraid to admit that this part of the process can be really difficult. It sucks!

Poet, painter, and Nobel Prize–winning novelist Hermann Hesse spoke about one's search for authenticity, self-knowledge, and spirituality, and described isolation as something that threatens our journey but that is *necessary* to achieve a deeper connection with Self and, ironically, a deeper connection with others:

We must become so alone, so utterly alone, that we withdraw into our innermost Self. It is a way of bitter suffering. But then our solitude is overcome, we are no longer alone, for we find that our inner-most Self is the spirit, that it is God, the indivisible. And suddenly we find ourselves in the midst of the world, yet undisturbed by its multiplicity, for in our inner-most soul we know ourselves to be one with all being.

This is why inauthentic individuals cannot stand diversity, inclusion, or differences in general. They have not found themselves amidst the world or pulled on the common thread of humanity. It's why they do not resonate with others, and why we may not relate to *them*.

Drawback #3: Grief

In growth, or any change, there is always loss. There is a lot to mourn during this journey of Self—relationships, dreams, and the many identities that we've shed along the way. We may be asked to grieve the previous versions of ourselves who chose the comfort of sidestepping consequences and the self-ishness of avoiding responsibility. We may be asked to grieve the people in whom we have invested. We may have to mourn the ignorance that allowed us to avoid our pain. We may have to mourn our previous beliefs, values, or morals.

But change is a double-sided coin—one side has loss, the other opportunity. It's an *opportunity* for people to meet us all over again and for us to get to finally meet our Self. It's an opportunity for greater intimacy. Within the grief, we can look for *space* that has been created by the loss. The space that can now—or whenever we're ready—be filled with things that are "right" for us.

For many of my clients, what appears to be the most painful part of grief is the realization that they did not show up for their Self the way they needed to, and the acknowledgment of the many ways in which they have disappointed or failed their Self along the way. To an extent, it's grieving one's own humanity. But as cliché as it sounds, "to err is human." Throughout this process, we need to mourn our unrealistic expectations of growth. Despite the hype, the process of authenticity is not purely pleasant.

Authenticity will not relieve you from being human and making mistakes. Authenticity does not bypass grief. Authenticity is not about numbing painful moments or distancing yourself from your past. It's not about "positive vibes," overinflation of our qualities, or forced self-love. Most important, authenticity is not about denying parts of your Self. On the contrary, it is about *you*. It's about feeling and experiencing your Self, others, the world—all of it. It's about what you *do* and how you choose to exist. It's about how you choose to use your time. It's about accepting and being gentle with the parts that feel broken, honoring your wounds. It is about holding your Self, seeing your Self. It's the process of gradually learning to accept and love who you are. It's about being informed but not transformed by the pain. It's about creating who you want to become.

It is only within tension or discomfort that change occurs, even necessary and desirable change. Since authenticity is the process of perpetual transformation, a journey of unending becoming, it involves learning to exist within the ache, the complexity, the undetermined, and the loss.

PRACTICE YOUR AGENCY

We are all asked by our communities to behave and "be" in a way that is acceptable and desirable to others. There is a wide range of demands set in place, all determined by people other than us. Oftentimes we are rewarded for being resilient, kind, successful, obedient, unique, happy, and attractive. And yet, these qualities tend to be lauded only to the degree to which they are deemed convenient, pleasant, or, unfortunately, advantageous. We are expected to be "enough"—whatever that means—in order for people to like us, but "not *too* much," which might make them feel threatened, insecure, triggered, or envious. The worst part is, we can't even just walk away. We have to exist within society. So, ultimately we must use our freedom, take responsibility, and make choices that will honor *us,* despite the expectations and demands of others.

In my late teens and early twenties, I surrounded myself with people who didn't genuinely see me, who didn't appreciate me for anything other than my achievements or utility, and didn't always treat me with respect. They liked that I invited them to fun events or gave them study notes. As I began to resist their expectations, they began to resist the "new" me. I was terrified of the isolation, but eventually it seemed better than the pain and exhaustion of trying to be someone I wasn't.

The truth was, impending loss was much greater and more threatening than the discomfort of resistance, and I felt true liberation when I deliberately worked on embracing who I was. And some of the aspects of myself that provoked the most resistance in others (my sensitivity, emotionality, and ambition) are, today, the very qualities that embody who I *am*. I learned an important lesson over time, a lesson I hope will be of help to you: Others don't get to tell you who you are or who you will become. *It's not their responsibility, it's yours.*

Hard Truth

If we allow the expectations and validations of other people to guide our actions, we allow them to mold who we become.

Gentle Reminder

Give yourself permission to become who you want to be and do it for your Self, not for others.

CHAPTER 6

Where Do I End and Others Begin?

From age nine—when I immigrated to Canada—I grew up in the Pacific Northwest. When people learn this fact, they are prone to make assumptions about what I'm like based on the stereotypes of the region. They automatically expect me to be a certain "type" of person—one who spends her weekends hiking, canoeing, or camping; one who makes organic fruit smoothies and eats granola for breakfast; one for whom activewear is the go-to aesthetic (or clothing made out of hemp or perhaps a chunky wool); they assume that I tend to a home garden; and then—and this one is always somewhat of a challenge for them to "discern"—I am either a die-hard Starbucks enthusiast or an independent coffee shop snob. Depending on how dedicated they are to the cause of not bothering to know me, they will also assume things about my past, my family, my income, my political views, and/or my faith.

All of this from one simple fact: where I grew up. It's fascinating how the mind has been trained to work—to pre-judge. At some point, it becomes absurd to watch people construct an image of us without even asking us to be in it. It took me years to realize that it was not about me (well, *obviously*), but that they needed me to be *that* person for *them*. I was the "object" in their existence that they needed to categorize, label, and ultimately "define" in order to decrease their anxiety of the unknown and make sense of the world.

For a long time, I was bothered by the assumptions people made, even if they were fairly innocuous. Not solely because they were inaccurate, but because every time I showed up as my Self, they seemed disappointed. I wasn't who they wanted me to be. They acted as if I had let them down simply by wanting, needing, or valuing the things that were important to me. They acted as if I inconvenienced them somehow—frowning or rolling their eyes as they tried to "accommodate" my presence. Or—worse yet—shaming me with passive-aggressive comments. "Ugh, it's so frustrating when people think they are too good for things." Oh, and my favorite: "If immigrants don't like the way things are done here, they should just go home."

It was disheartening, confusing, and ultimately an intensely lonely experience. Their assumptions and expectations left no room for me; they had filled in all the blanks. I was then left with the *task* of showing up in a way that would validate their narrative about me. Even if I could have fulfilled their expectations, I wouldn't have. But the truth was, I *couldn't*—for one, I grew up in a family that couldn't afford organic vegetables or expensive activewear, and second, I had spent too long being scared and fighting for my life to spend precious moments making excuses for my own existence.

I felt like "they" were infringing on my sense of Self. They were violating my most sacred of boundaries by knowingly (or unknowingly) coercing me to be an extension of *their* inner world. They didn't give me permission or space to show up. They didn't bother to *see* me.

This may not seem like a big deal, and I was honestly tempted to present a more "shocking" and "bigger" example, but that would go against the entire point of this book. It's not just moments of extreme oppression that lead to us to feeling violated. A dramatic example would mislead you to think that self-loss is easy to notice and always unfolds dramatically. It's also in those difficult-to-spot or easy-to-dismiss moments filled with small assumptions, impositions, or resistance to our preferences that we struggle to *live* who we are.

In my late twenties, it almost felt like an act of rebellion to show people my philosophy-reading, city-loving, croissant-eating, photograph-taking, tennis-playing, Paris Fashion Week–watching, nomadic Self. I decided, and have kept deciding, that I was going to express my Self. I decided that I would unmistakably show who I was, and if other people still didn't see me, I knew it was because they didn't want to.

Surprisingly to some, showing my Self did not mean having more heart-to-heart conversations, sharing more of my painful life experiences, producing a beautiful piece of art, or posting more pictures or confessions on social media. That didn't work for me because 1) the people around me weren't looking or listening closely enough, and 2) the relationships didn't feel safe enough for me to be vulnerable.

So, the way I showed myself was by setting boundaries.

We often don't connect self-expression and boundaries, but

indeed, boundaries are a vital form of self-expression—and, in my case, they were the *most* effective form of self-expression. If you are curious about what they sounded like for me, here are some examples:

- "No thanks. I don't feel like camping."
- "Making jokes about me being a 'princess' is hurting my feelings. Please stop."
- "I would rather go grab a croissant instead of a salad. I'll meet you guys after."
- "I appreciate your input, but ultimately I have decided to travel for the next couple of years."
- "If I need advice on my choice of clothing, I will ask for it."
- "I will not tolerate derogatory comments about my heritage."
- "I don't want to get married right now. If I change my mind, I will let you know."
- "I am not sure I want kids. I need you to stop asking when I will have them."
- "I don't feel comfortable sharing about my war experiences, but thank you for asking."
- "I don't feel comfortable with you looking through my phone."
- "I am also struggling right now and can't be your primary support system."
- "If you yell or swear at me, this conversation will end."
- "I like to keep my romantic life private."
- "I don't like talking about people behind their backs. Let's change the topic."

- "I know you're upset, but I don't feel it's my place to get involved."
- "You don't have to like my profession, but I need you to talk about it with respect."
- "If you're more than twenty minutes late, I will have to go without you."
- "I am not comfortable with you commenting on my body."
- "I will reply to your email after the weekend."
- "No, I am not going to share what my therapist said."

Do you feel like you understand me more? Just because you heard what I *won't* do, or what I *won't* accept? My guess is yes. It's fascinating how that happens. I didn't tell you what I liked, I didn't give you any facts about my life, and yet you still got a glimpse of me. That's because, if I share my boundaries with you, I am not just telling you about my needs, wants, or expectations; I am showing you **who I am and how I understand myself.**

THE OUTLINE OF THE SELF: WHAT *ARE* BOUNDARIES?

I know that most of us have heard about boundaries because psychology has been very vocal about the concept lately, and it seems everyone on social media is talking about them. But, just to make sure we are all on the same page, here is a quick overview:

- Boundaries are guidelines (not ultimatums).
- Boundaries enhance understanding and safety in a relationship.

- Boundaries are a way to take care of our Self.
- Boundaries need to be communicated clearly.
- Boundaries often come with consequences if they are violated.
- Boundaries can be divided into six main areas:
  1. physical
  2. sexual
  3. emotional
  4. intellectual
  5. material
  6. time
- Boundaries are relevant in every relationship (even— and especially—in good ones).
- Boundaries are not about punishing or pushing people away. They are about creating a healthy distance that will help nurture both individuals in a relationship (and the relationship itself, if applicable).

I find that most descriptions and teachings on boundaries fall short in one regard: a lack of emphasis on the relationship between our boundaries and our sense of Self. **We cannot separate our boundaries from our sense of Self.** Why? Because **healthy boundaries are an outline of who we are.** Boundaries don't just nurture relationships and protect us, they *define* us. They are like a silhouette of who we are as a human, communicating with others in a way that helps them see and understand us.

In my profession, I see so many individuals struggling to set and keep boundaries regardless of the fact that they have read *all* of the books and taken *all* of the workshops. The reality is that unless someone really *knows* who they are, they are fated to misuse or struggle with boundaries. *We can't outline the shape of something if we don't know where the edges are, and what it looks like.* Boundaries are predicated on knowing who we are, what we need, what we want, what we expect, and what our worldview is. Boundaries are one of the quickest ways for individuals to tell us about the beliefs they hold about themselves or their work, relationships, family, faith, body, etc. **People can lie, but boundaries seldom do.**

In fact, poor boundaries are often an indication of a weak sense of Self. Seems harsh, I know. Hear me out. Any context that would lead to us not knowing how to set boundaries, or not feeling safe enough to set boundaries, is a context that would threaten our sense of Self. Not *always,* but often the two biggest stumbling blocks in setting boundaries are lack of self-understanding and lack of seriousness (which often go hand in hand when we don't respect our Self).

Trying to set boundaries before knowing our Self is like looking over our shoulder in math class and writing down an answer to an equation that's not even on our test. It might be the right answer for *an* equation, but not *your* equation. In order for boundaries to be meaningful or helpful, we need to feel a deep sense of alignment with them, and they need to work on a practical level. For example, one person may have set a boundary to establish that they are unavailable for anyone after 9:00 P.M., but if you are, say, an ER doctor or a new mother, it won't be realistic for you to set that boundary. If you were to try to abide by this boundary, chances are you would have to change some major aspects of your life (and as a result, you would end up changing your Self). In order to change our boundaries, we have to change something about our Self—boundaries are a natural extension of who we are. Our Self is a work of art; our boundaries are our frame.

Another example: In order to implement a new relationship boundary, like "I am not okay with you repeatedly canceling on me at the last minute" or "If you don't stop yelling at me, I will leave," we *must* believe that we are worthy of respect. As long as we don't believe we deserve better, we won't ask for it, and we will allow our boundaries to keep being violated. In order to implement a boundary (especially one that we will stick to), it must come from an authentic space—a choice to utilize our freedom in a way that's responsible for who we are. We are responsible to act as the Self, and to protect the Self.

If the Self is truly ever-changing and evolving, it means that—to an extent—so are our boundaries. We are not just drawing a silhouette; we are drawing a motion picture that reflects our growth as well as our specific context from moment to moment. It is our responsibility to check in with our Self and choose boundaries that fit. When our relationships, beliefs, or settings change, often, so do our boundaries. This is not about being flaky, it's about maintaining *attunement*. When I am doing a Q&A in front of an audience, the questions I choose to answer will be different than when I am having drinks with my friends. In both contexts, boundaries are crucial.

For many, the lack of taking boundaries seriously is a stumbling block because they don't understand what is at stake and, as a consequence, they don't set boundaries with conviction. That was me. I used to *kind of, sort of, maybe* allude to something that I needed . . . but that was before I realized that the combination of other people's demands and my lack of boundaries left me feeling *lost*. It was not until my panic attack that I accepted the fact that my lack of boundaries had exacerbated the issues I was having in relationships, with my mental health, and with my lack of understanding of who I was. *The scribbly doodles I had drawn weren't a clear enough outline of my Self for others to see—they weren't even distinct enough for me to recognize my Self.*

OVERCORRECTING

We've all overcorrected at some point in our lives. If the last time we went to the beach it was extremely windy, next time we are likely to bring a jacket and a blanket even though the forecast says calm and sunny. If we were rude to someone during a previous hangout, we will try to be especially, and perhaps unnaturally, nice the next time. If someone tells us we've gained some weight, we may lose an absurd amount just so we never have to hear that again (even though a conversation like that probably shouldn't have happened in the first place). If we lose a partner because we suffocated them (figuratively), we may not pay enough attention to our next one.

This is totally normal. Usually, overcorrection follows an unpleasant experience or a loss. We don't want to repeat either, so we try to protect ourselves by going as far as we can in the opposite direction. I see this in therapy all the time, especially when a client learns a new skill, such as boundary-setting. I always applaud their enthusiasm and commitment, but often I have to remind them to keep their approach realistic and leave room for the messy humanity of other people.

A while ago, I had such a conversation with a client in her early twenties. When she first came to therapy, she wanted help grieving the end of a three-year relationship and figuring out who she was without it. The grieving process often requires facing a lot of difficult questions, such as "Why did this happen, what could I have done differently, and what can I learn from this?" Ultimately, she realized that her lack of boundaries and lack of self-understanding greatly contributed to the dissolution of the relationship. She was very introspective, willing to learn, and committed. Once we broached the topic of boundaries, she began implementing them immediately.

Fast-forward to a year later; the client started to casually see someone new. She seemed happy, and said it felt like a perfect match. Surprisingly, about four months into dating, she came to a session to read me a breakup text she had drafted. She had written that they couldn't keep seeing each other because she had made it clear in the past that she was not okay with being sent texts while she was visiting her mother, who was sick, at the hospital, and he had texted her while she was there. For context, the client had made it clear that during visitation hours on Sundays she wanted to have no distractions, to be fully present and there for her mom. The day that her partner violated her no-texting boundary, he sent a message that said: "I know today you're getting your mom's test results back. Thinking of you!" Because of this, she was upset and ready to end things. She had been so scared to enter another relationship in which her needs and preferences were ignored or unseen, that any indication of this became a deal-breaker. She'd begun to use boundaries *as a wall instead of a blueprint*.

We took a deep breath together and I asked if her boundaries were becoming rigid. We explored the idea that perhaps repeating the boundary might be a more appropriate course of action than ending the relationship. Or maybe, just maybe, it was okay for her to enjoy the attention and care she was receiving for the first time in a long time—maybe that boundary was no longer as necessary or important as it had been in the past? Only she knew the best way to move forward, of course, but I was there to help her explore her experience. Ultimately, she decided to reiterate the boundary rather than end the relationship. She also chose to communicate to her partner that although this was a kind gesture, it triggered her and she was struggling to accept it.

It took time, but eventually she released her fear and learned to accept the good things in her life. She broke the habit of constantly seeing and anticipating the worst in every situation.

WHEN THE LINE IS CROSSED

When someone violates our boundaries, we often respond with resentment, disappointment, hurt, or anger. We may initially try to justify the person's poor behavior, blame ourselves for allowing them to cross our boundaries, feel ashamed by the way we are being treated, or start doubting our decisions. But when their actions feel like a barrier or an impediment to being our Self—when we feel unseen, unappreciated, or treated unfairly—we draw boundaries as part of our protective reaction. We set a reflexive boundary, or coping reaction, **as a means to prevent being further wounded and lost**. The aim is to find a way to bear our hurt or protect our Self from it. In order to get a sense of how you react to your boundaries being violated, let me ask you three simple questions:

- How do you behave in contexts where you don't feel like you can be yourself?
- What is your first impulse when you feel that you are being treated unfairly?
- What do you do when you feel like you're constantly being overlooked, outvoted, ignored, or not genuinely seen?

Your actions, my guess would be, are the reflexive boundaries I am talking about—the coping reactions—that allow you to bear your hurt. These boundaries or self-adjustments are not always intentional or grounded in self-awareness. Arguably, they are also not a long-term solution and have the potential of being maladaptive.

In existential analysis, coping reactions fall into four categories:

1. Distancing
2. Overactivity
3. Aggression
4. Freezing

All of these responses have the same goal in mind—to protect us from harm—they just approach it differently.

1. Distancing

When we feel violated or imposed upon, we tend to distance ourselves from others and/or the pain with which we are confronted. The goal of distancing is ultimately to preserve our sense of Self by not participating in situations that threaten it. However, by the act of distancing, we may also unknowingly draw boundaries that single us out, risk relational ruptures, and lead to loneliness. *Here are some common distancing behaviors:*

- **Walking away.** People walk away when they are unclear about how to proceed with an interaction without feeling unsafe. By walking away, we have decided that we can, in fact, live without whatever is presenting itself. It's a form of rejection and a statement: *You can choose to proceed, but not with me.* It's a boundary created by physically removing one's Self.

  I've never actually walked away from a conversation, but I've had a person do it to me. It didn't feel great, to say the least, but I would guess that they'd say the same. If someone is walking away, chances are that they no longer feel like they can coexist with us. People may have endless discussions about who's to blame for that occurring, but the most important question is: "How did the dynamic turn into a space where the Self could no longer exist because it felt emotionally threatened by being wounded or unseen?"

- **Tapping out.** Taking ourselves out of the conversation by withdrawing and being silent is a very common coping response. But did you ever think about it in terms of boundaries? We choose (i.e., set a boundary) to no longer engage or give of our Self. Silence can be incredibly passive-aggressive and unhealthy, but it's often a sign that the person feels like they can no longer participate without jeopardizing their Self.

Another tactic, a less obvious approach to tapping out, is distracting the other person from the matter at hand by jumping from subject to subject or disguising the problem. You might notice your tendency to do this when someone brings up a difficult topic during a family dinner (like, say, the fact that you're single) and you have the inclination to distract them by talking about a sale you saw at Target or your recent promotion. I sometimes notice this with clients. They will bring up a difficult topic to discuss, but then quickly switch to something that's clearly less pressing as a way to self-regulate. Being aware of this pattern can help us realize when we are feeling overwhelmed, triggered, or unsafe. It can help us replace our reflexive boundaries with intentional ones.

Being formal. Formality is a common way for us to create distance. When we first meet someone, we often behave more formally because there is a lack of familiarity, safety, or understanding. When we reintroduce formality in our relationships, it is a way of reestablishing a boundary and creating the amount of distance we want to have between them and us.

You know how when, after a breakup, you see the other person in public and are stiff and polite, calling them by their name instead of "honey"? You now end your emails with "All the best" instead of "Love." Being formal is a way of saying, *We are no longer close.* It's keeping someone at arm's length in order to protect ourselves.

- **Perceiving insults as a joke.** It's hard to deny that laughter and humor have a positive impact on our mental health. However, when we constantly use humor to defuse situations or distance ourselves from pain, it can prevent us from truly facing our reality. Simply put: Treating something (or someone) as a joke is a way of not taking it (or them) seriously. In these instances we are setting a boundary by indirectly conveying, *What you are saying can't be true because if it were, it would be too cruel.* So instead, we laugh off any hurtful remarks as a way to not have to deal with the pain we would feel if we approached the situation seriously.

- **Over-identifying with another person's point of view.** This happens when our attempt to understand someone else goes so far that we lose sight of our own experience—intentionally or unintentionally. We do this in an effort to distance ourselves from our own feelings, thoughts, or needs. Even wonderful things like compassion and sympathy—if unchecked—can lead us to self-abandon for others.

Let's say you have an argument with your partner. It could be that they want you to give up your apartment and move in together, and you are not ready to. Or it could be that they want to get married and you don't believe in marriage. Whatever the problem, you decide to do what *they* want and then you find your Self in a context that challenges who you are. It becomes a threat to your sense of Self, because your actions no longer align with how you understand your Self. These are simple examples of what can happen when we start to erase our own outline and expand it to incorporate someone else. Sometimes we try to force their beliefs and desires to become our own. Sometimes we feel that stretching our boundaries is safer than making them smaller—but, sometimes it's not. Sometimes we overextend in a relationship and, as a result, we lose our Self within it.

2. Overactivity

Overactivity is our attempt to make space for our Self and move forward by ostensibly skipping, running away from, or jumping over whatever is hurting or threatening us. We also tend to overlook ourselves in an effort (and hope) to be seen and recognized by others.

It often manifests as a go-getter mentality. You may clean constantly, belong to a bunch of clubs, strive for perfection (so no one can complain or fault you), stay distracted by constantly being "busy" in order to impress others and increase your value in their eyes. But you are functioning almost like a cog in a machine, acting, having little to no inner experience. You are so busy that you don't interact with or respond to what is really going on for you. You become like a shell that has no concern for—or even awareness of—the animal that lives within it. If this coping mechanism could talk, according to Längle, it would sound something like: "I need to constantly be doing something visible in order to legitimate myself for others, so that I can *live*!" Instead of stepping back or tapping out, as we do when we distance our Self, this reaction sends us barreling forward, becoming *more* active as a way to cope with the threat. This is not that different from people-pleasing: It is focusing on, or conforming to, the other in order to avoid genuine encounters. We want recognition from others because we cannot offer it to our Self.

People who are overactive often seek attention through the way they speak, dress, and move through the world. They have, like all of us, a desire to be seen, a yearning for someone to acknowledge the fact that they exist. This does not come from a place of self-centeredness; it's from a place of self-preservation. They are also more likely to "play along" or give in to the other person even when they are feeling hurt and wronged. They may identify with the aggressor, laugh along at their painful jokes, perhaps even agree with them. This is because, if they have a sense of *belonging* (whether it's warranted or not), they may feel protected from being discarded or lost.

3. Aggression

When we feel threatened, it's not uncommon to display aggression. This can look like being intolerant, oppositional, indignant, demanding, or violating other people's physical boundaries. The main purpose is to stand (metaphorically or physically) against something. The aim of being aggressive is often to be seen and taken seriously in order to avoid being further hurt. It's like when we make a loud sound when someone bumps into us in a crowded subway, as a way to signal our presence and prevent being shoved again. If we could speak with clarity in those moments, according to Längle, it would sound like: "Please look at me. I am here and I am suffering. Can you please stop?"

I often see aggression emerge at the point at which someone finds the situation outrageous ("How *dare* they? How *could* they? I will *never* let this happen to me again!"). When we have felt a deep sense of injustice or a sense of degradation that does not allow us to be a person, we fight back—"I won't be treated this way!" We turn our internal emotions into something that *feels* like external action.

First, aggression emerges—then the instinct to fight. We need to remember that anger yearns to be *seen*. Unlike sadness, which often wants to hide, anger evokes a sense of self-expression. Aggression typically emerges from a deep sense of powerlessness and leads to a desire to "run down" (destroy) the threat. When the aggressive impulse is combined with a sense of "justice," meaning we feel we have the "right" to lash out, we begin to punish others. It's a way to harm the offender in order to offset the injustice (vengeance). It's also about "teaching" someone a lesson, even if that someone is us. Aggression is not always obvious. During one of my existential analysis workshops, a professor once told us that sarcasm is often a socially acceptable form of aggression—*oof,* that struck deep. I used to be very sarcastic (*all* my jokes were steeped in it), and that was the first time it dawned on me that I was actually angry.

I see an act of anger as a desperate plea for acknowledgment. It's a (misdirected) way to assert ourselves, to take up space, and to draw boundaries in relation to the other. It's a way to establish or reestablish boundaries so that no one can step over us. The intention is good, but the execution is often poor.

When my clients feel anger or aggression building up, I ask them to reflect on the following three questions:

- What need is not being met?
- What part of me feels threatened?
- What boundary is being violated?

Unless we become *aware* of what is going on for us, we will continue to protect ourselves by being destructive rather than productive.

4. Freezing

Freezing occurs when we feel unable to act. It's when we cannot stand something to such an extreme degree that we experience paralysis or loss of feelings. A lighter form of this would be being stunned by an insult or offense that is directly perceived as a threat to our worth. We may become "speechless" when we are not invited to an event, when someone forgets to buy us a Christmas gift, or when we speak in a group and no one responds. It's the feeling of being neglected and not knowing how to move forward.

A more painful form of this violation would result in feeling hurt, and when that happens, we tend to turn away from people. If someone rejects us, ignores our boundaries, or belittles us (especially repeatedly), we may feel a *wounding of our honor*. It is a deeper wounding and one that causes inner suffering. A relationship fracture of this type—one that we don't know how to address—can actually inflict psychosomatic reactions such as migraines or stomach/digestion issues.

Other, more severe forms of freezing are: being unable to speak, shamefully hiding one's needs, waiting for the threat to pass, embitterment, denying our feelings, forgetting events, dissociating, depersonalizing. These responses are often a result of severe trauma, and not a common, everyday threat of self-loss.

Stop and think for a moment: What do your reflexive boundaries tell you about who you are?

It's amazing—the effort our minds put forth to neutralize the obstructions to being our Self. But even our best attempts don't always lead to the desired outcome. What we *can* do is help our Self out by setting *conscious* (not coping) boundaries that can eliminate the threat and build safety with the people around us.

Before setting a boundary, ask yourself:

- Why am I setting this boundary?
- What is my goal with this boundary?
- Does this boundary promote my well-being?
- Does this boundary resonate with who I am?
- Is this boundary respectful of who I am?
- What/who am I protecting with this boundary?
- Does this boundary promote healthy relationships?
- Which of my core beliefs is the foundation for this boundary?

- Is this the best way to word this boundary?
- When is the best time to set this boundary?
- What is the consequence if someone violates my boundary?

Often the biggest obstacle around boundaries—affecting both our willingness to set them and others' readiness to accept them—is our understanding of what they are. Boundaries are often understood as a form of rejection or threat, rather than a sketch we can offer others to deepen their understanding of our Self. It is a frame within which their understanding of us will unfold over time, a frame that will protect the precious process of our Being.

Hard Truth

The weaker your boundaries, the weaker your sense of Self.

Gentle Reminder

Boundaries are a love language. Let's treat them as such.

PART III

The Self You Live

I have been and still am a seeker, but I have ceased to question stars and books. I have begun to listen to the teaching my blood whispers to me. Mine is not a pleasant story, it does not possess the gentle harmony of invented tales; like the lives of all men who have given up trying to deceive themselves, it is a mixture of nonsense and chaos, madness and dreams.

—HERMANN HESSE, *DEMIAN*

CHAPTER 7

Mental Decluttering

Create Space for Who You Really Are

I consider myself a minimalist. All—and I mean *all*—of my earthly belongings fit in one large suitcase and a standard-size carry-on. This was not always the case—my quest for minimalism began seven years ago on one cold, miserable February afternoon in Berlin. The dark skies threatened a second downpour of rain, and only a few people were out. No one bothered to look up as I dragged my oversized luggage across the cobblestones, or when I tripped and my suitcases fell and my purse emptied of its belongings, leaving my wallet, keys, passport, and electronics spread across the wet sidewalk. No one stopped to help. People just kept on walking around me, ignoring my struggle. And of course, I acted like nothing was wrong as I scrambled to gather my things. Life is just like that sometimes, I guess—we suffer and neither we nor those around us bother to acknowledge it.

Breathless, I finally made it to the entrance of a train station. And, since it was Europe, there were no elevators or escalators. Just me, the stairs, and my massive bags. Two trips up and down and several hardy knocks to the ankles later, I made it to the right platform. But the door didn't care that half of my suitcase wasn't on the train as it began to mercilessly close. The other passengers shot me nasty looks, and so, aside from being sweaty and frustrated, I was now also humiliated. (Why is it that the person struggling is the one who's embarrassed? Shouldn't the people who don't help feel self-conscious?)

After this, I swore to *never* travel with more than I could carry. I was ready to declutter and minimize my entire life, not just my possessions. I wanted to move with freedom and space that I did not have. I was ready for my life's metaphor to no longer be that I had "too much baggage." It was a stereotype, and I hated that.

As I purged my external possessions, I began to notice that I had more internal space—it became easier to breathe, to make decisions. First I donated, sold, or threw out all the things that I no longer needed (and that no longer fit into one suitcase). Then, I began to go through the storage at my parents' house. I got rid of old yearbooks, blankets, movie stubs, and random gifts from family friends. I hesitated throwing out that one bridesmaid dress I could wear again if the royal family invited me to the ball, all those Juicy Couture sweatpants in case the early 2000s were ever to make a fashion comeback (perhaps they have already?), or that skirt I bought for "when I lose weight." And what about all the handmade gifts or random letters from my ex? What if we got back together? My mental space was taken up by clutter that consisted of hypotheticals—the *what-if*s, regrets, and "maybes" of life. That was far more damaging than the storage boxes. Ultimately, going through my things allowed me to clear out the corners of my mind.

Much like when I got rid of a redundant itchy wool sweater to make space in my suitcase, I decided to stop thinking about the opinions people had about my pending divorce. Mental decluttering, for me, meant eliminating anything I spent time or energy on that no longer served or aligned with me. *It was making space for my Self.* Mental decluttering can include, but is not limited to, the releasing of thoughts, beliefs, assumptions, roles, habits, fears, relationships, or possessions— ideally the ones that are not serving us. It's about getting rid of anything that does not assist us in *being* in the world in a way that feels true to who we are, and who we want to be.

I think minimalism is often confused with the act of restricting one's Self. But for me, having less (physically and mentally) meant choosing *not* to be restricted; it was a task of preserving my will, creating space, and, consequently, using my freedom. By having less, I felt like I could give my Self more space *to be*.

Space is what gives us freedom because, existentially speaking, space is where we can exist—literally and figuratively. So it stands to reason that without space, we cease to exist. Space is what presents us with the opportunity to decide, to act, to move, to grow, to realize our potential. A famous quote often attributed to Viktor Frankl describes this perfectly: "Between stimulus and response there is a space. In that space is our power to choose our response. In our response lies our growth and our freedom." If we don't use our space, we are stripping away our autonomy and power and, consequently, we risk losing our Self.

Space is not just something that's given; space is something we *take and create*.

When we feel like we have no space, we stop offering it to others. It creates a vicious cycle. We cannot let others "be" if we don't have enough space to let our Self "be," and vice versa. We feel that the space they take up is infringing on the space we *need* to show up. So, before responding to an infuriating text message from a colleague or a friend—or before you react to your partner not unloading the dishwasher . . . yet again—*take* the time to reflect on what's happening for you and how you want to show up in that moment. *Use the space* to think about who you are and want to be. Space is what allows us to be deliberate—and when life becomes busy, this is when we tend to become reactive or careless and, well, lost.

Decisions are our intentional responses to life; reactions are impulsive actions usually grounded in pain, fear, insecurities, or wounds. Space lets us step back and look at all the possibilities that are not limited to the current moment or feeling. It gives us perspective and grounding.

Without distance, we can't see the forest for the trees, so to speak.

There are many ways we can create space and distance for ourselves. For one, we can do it with our imagination. I once heard that while Frankl was in the concentration camp, he imagined himself after the war speaking to audiences about his experiences—and he ended up doing just that. Some other ways include breathing deeply, moving our body through physical activities, taking breaks or "sleeping on it" in order to come back from a *different* space, finding humor and irony in hard things, or simply saying *no*.

For me, space was about creating physical distance from people and places that made it difficult for me to be intentional and authentic. What started as decluttering to the point that all my possessions fit into a couple of bags turned into packing those bags and traveling the world. Ever since my own existential crisis and the divorce that followed, I've essentially lived as a nomad. The act of creating space is exactly why I began to travel in the first place. I had a problem I needed to solve—well, two actually: I was deeply unhappy, and I had no idea who I was.

And while traveling to "find ourselves" or "get away" from things has become a cliché (and is steeped in privilege), it makes sense. We are seeking more space in which we can exist, especially if we feel like we are in a context that doesn't allow us to. The need to look for space in foreign contexts often occurs when we haven't taken the initiative to create it in our lives and current situations (or when, for various reasons, we *feel* like we are truly unable to take the initiative). Often, our contexts are saturated with expectation, opinions, people, and routines that leave no space for, well, *space*. We begin to operate on autopilot. We go through entire days without much intention or awareness.

There's a reason people are sometimes advised to quit an ingrained habit (like smoking) while they're in a new environment. It's because in a new space, we become more conscious. There isn't the ten-minute break at the same time every day in which we mindlessly grab our pack of cigarettes, make an instant coffee, and go stand in front of the building to smoke.

Being in a new context allows us a moment to *think* before we do something, because we are no longer operating automatically within our daily routine. It creates space for decisions that are more than just habit. It's a way of reclaiming and using our freedom.

Sometimes the act of moving is not running away—it's running *toward*. Traveling gave me space and distance, allowing me to *be* with my problems and address them. I began to discern my Self from the problem, realizing I was more than my sorrow, my anxiety, or my "failed" relationships. The truth is, once we identify our Self as separate from the problem, we win our Self back by becoming empowered and—don't forget—still bearing responsibility for who we are.

WHY WE STRUGGLE TO LET GO

Oftentimes, it's difficult to release *things* because we assign meaning to possessions that doesn't belong there. This was the case for me. I'd attached so much meaning and safety to physical possessions that I wasn't intentional about creating meaning and safety within myself.

Having possessions is not inherently an issue, but the relationships we form with our possessions can be problematic. Letting go can be particularly tricky for people who at some point didn't have their needs met, or who grew up lacking things. As a child during the war, the essentials—such as food—were scarce. My family's nonessentials were nonexistent. This wasn't "minimalism"; it was trauma. We didn't feel liberated and filled with space, we felt vulnerable and unsafe. We were robbed of things we needed and cared for.

As a result, my family members tightened their grip on their possessions. Not because they thought material things necessarily had value, but because not having to experience what it's like being without them did. They saved every article of clothing or half-filled can of hairspray because maybe, just maybe, they would need it again. And even once they could afford to buy a new T-shirt or pillow, the mindset was difficult to change.

I remember moving into my college dorm with a car filled to the brim, still unhappy that I couldn't bring everything I "needed." As ridiculous as it seems to me now, I know that that version of myself was yearning to have familiar things around her during an unfamiliar transition. It was about a feeling of safety, not about that half-burned candle I brought even though I could never light it, as per dormitory regulations. That candle reminded me of home. That bright, hand-made blanket that clashed with everything else in my room reminded me of falling in love for the first time. And the wooden toy boat represented my last vacation (ten years prior) with my dad, a man I loved but rarely got to see. I was worried that if I didn't keep these things, it would make my previous experiences less real. I needed proof of my life, and this is why I was so protective of my items—they were souvenirs of the versions of myself that I could no longer fully grasp, that no longer existed.

Recently, a friend asked me a very common, albeit thought-provoking, question: "If your house was on fire, what would you run in and get?"

My answer, after a long pause, was: "Nothing."

Truly, I can think of nothing I would risk my life for, nothing external that I feel that I absolutely need. I feel the same way when my bag doesn't show up after my flight lands and I see the sheepish look on the customer service person at the airport who is failing to explain where it is. Often I'm annoyed at first, but then I feel liberated. My house is my soul, not brick and mortar, or a suitcase filled to the brim.

So let me ask you: If your house was on fire, what would you run in and get? What is so important that you would risk your precious Self?

There is a crucial difference between our possession of things and our possession of Self. Decluttering our lives can feel threatening, because it's a form of deconstruction. It's an approach to understanding everything that comprises who we are—and who we are not—by unraveling and untangling our habits, beliefs, relationships, and wounds. We must first deconstruct in order to choose how we want to construct our Self—**and the only way to create our Self is to make space for who we are.** It's time to release the actions, beliefs, habits, and perspectives that do not truly belong to us.

Expectations

Most of us—arguably all of us to an extent—have an inclination to allow other people's expectations to impact us and shape how we think about our Self, what choices we make, and who we become. Unknowingly, we often experience a competition of needs: *Do I fulfill my need to be my Self or do I fulfill my need to belong and be loved?*

When we are unclear about our *Self,* we welcome the clarity that comes from other people's projections (good or bad) because it satisfies the unknown. Our brain is more intimidated by an unknown than an inaccurate known, so it would rather misclassify or generalize our Self based on other people's narratives than embrace the space of not fully understanding who we are. How we understand our Self dictates our actions (and the space we take up in in the world), so this tendency puts us at risk for becoming something that *other* people want or believe us to be.

Before I faced my own self-loss, I spent so much of my time *actively being* who others needed and wanted me to be that, eventually, I created an inauthentic version of myself.

I'll never forget one afternoon when I had a sudden anxiety attack during an important meeting at work. I can't remember what sparked it, but suddenly the stress became so overwhelming that I blacked out. I literally lost consciousness for several seconds. Not a single person noticed. Then, as the meeting was dispersing, a colleague came up to me. I was nervous. *Did she see? Was she questioning my competency?*

Nope. She wanted to praise my involvement in and contribution to the meeting. She said that one day she hoped to carry herself with the same self-assurance as me. She hoped to reach a point where she had it "all together"—like I did.

As I stared blankly at her, I saw the eager expectation in her eyes, and I recognized the image I needed to protect (for her). Awkwardly, I accepted the compliment, and she remained unaware that I just wanted to get away as soon as I could and google my symptoms in the car, that I wished I could be anyone *other* than myself at that moment. She helped me deny my own reality, and I then used her perception of my "success" as my own understanding of who I was.

If no one acknowledges that I am in pain, am I in pain? If no one sees that I'm lost, am I lost?

You want me to have it all together? Okay, I'll be someone who has it all together.

I became dedicated to perpetuating that false understanding of me. My head was constantly filled with noise about how I could keep up the act. Ultimately, it led to my misinterpreting of my own Self. I have to admit, at first I was relieved when my colleague did not recognize my distress, but then it sank in—*she didn't recognize my distress!* It was this realization that helped me get to a place where I decided to no longer care about what others wanted or expected. Why am I catering my life to people who don't see me? To people who are not experiencing what it's like to *be* me?

Sometimes, we place expectations on our Self (e.g., to be the one who has it all together, even when we most certainly do not). Other times we embody others' perceptions (e.g., being the "good girl"). The issue with living our lives based on expectations is that it's often not aligned with who we are. Sooner or later, we realize that losing our Self to fit a role—whether assigned by us or by others—is much too high a price. Expectations can be good, as long as they are realistic and aligned (e.g., I expect my Self to take responsibility for *all* my decisions).

Here are seven questions to ask in order to challenge and declutter the "shoulds" in your life:

1. Does this expectation resonate with who I am?
2. Does this expectation bring me closer to my desired future?
3. Does this expectation promote my well-being?

4. Does this expectation respect my needs?
5. Is this expectation realistic?
6. Who am I doing this for? And why?
7. Who has imposed these expectations?

Food for thought: If we focused as much on gaining our sense of Self as we do on our "shoulds," how would we structure our days differently? What would we spend our time thinking about? How would our actions vary? If we are choosing to take responsibility for who we are and who we will become, how will our thoughts, interactions, focus, and goals change?

Habits

Liz was thirty-four years old and living in New York City. It had been her dream ever since she was a teen. In her early twenties she made the move, worked terrible jobs, went on horrible dates, and paid astronomical rent—it was all part of the *experience*. Now she was in her mid-thirties with a thriving career, dream apartment, and fun social life. Drugs and excessive alcohol consumption were normalized and promoted within her circles. She was not particularly a big fan, but it seemed to be part of the package. Reluctantly at first, she participated, and then eventually she was doing cocaine and getting blackout drunk on a regular basis. She disliked this part of herself, but what started off as a rare social activity had become somewhat of a Friday night routine, and she didn't know how to get out of it. Eventually, she and her friends stopped making "official" plans and everyone would just show up at their favorite bar at eight, ready to party. I get it. It's like when my sister and I say, "Let's go grab food" and automatically just start walking toward our favorite Korean restaurant. It's a habit, muscle memory. But habits are routines that end up shaping us. Instead of surrendering to them, we need to inspect them:

- What habits did you adopt because of your surroundings?
- What habits do not support who you are and who you want to become?
- Do you have any habits that sabotage you or your growth?
- What habits nurture you?
- What habits are encouraged by others?

What we do is who we become. Habits are tendencies or practices that can become automatic to us. We've done them so many times that it's now second nature, or just nature, and they can bypass attunement and inner consent. Habits are an expression of who we are, and if we don't like our habits, we probably won't like ourselves. We can't do things we are ashamed of or don't respect, and expect to admire and appreciate our Self—just like we can't put in all the wrong ingredients and expect the cake to taste good.

There are many clearly destructive habits we may want to break, such as drinking when upset, smoking when drinking, or texting when drunk. But there are also other habits that may be worth breaking, such as:

- Basing our identity on our relationships with others
- Settling for less than we deserve

- Hiding our success for the sake of others
- Lying to keep peace
- Putting the needs of other people before our own
- Drinking as a means of dealing with emotional distress
- Apologizing for things that are not our fault
- Not enforcing our boundaries out of fear of rejection
- Denying our reality
- Betraying ourselves for the sake of a relationship
- Seeking external validation instead of internal validation
- Offering unsolicited advice

It's important to also remember that not all habits are bad. Healthy habits can help us create a routine that will promote the life we want and help normalize and internalize actions that can help us *be* who we want to be.

Some healthy habits may entail self-soothing instead of grabbing the phone to call someone to help us calm down, taking responsibility for our words and actions, apologizing quickly when we've made a mistake, not taking ourselves so seriously, and giving ourselves the space we need to feel and think. Healthy habits can also be practical things like calling our friends or family to check in, brushing our teeth, drinking water, and writing down things for which we are grateful.

Relationships

Like many of us, the area in which I most abandoned my Self was in my romantic relationships. I spent years trying to be someone I thought my partners wanted. I pretended to like watching hockey, to like dressing up in "sexy" clothes, to be "chill" about their various ambitions or lack thereof. I pretended my sex drive was higher than it was, that I enjoyed spending time with all their friends, that I was okay with them making snide remarks about my work, that I was okay with the unresolved feelings some of them had for their exes, that I was comfortable with them controlling who I hung out with. I pretended for so long that eventually I believed my own lies and was genuinely confused when I went to bed most nights frustrated, with tears in my eyes. My life—my existence—was filled with all of these traits and "preferences" that were not my own.

My marriage brought out the worst in me (or not-me?). I deflected attention from who I was and encouraged him to focus on the person he wanted me to be. He ended up being in a relationship with someone I had very little to do with, and I ended up being alone.

I wasn't present, which is why nothing about our relationship felt intimate. Even sex began to evoke a sense of disgust in me, and, as I later learned, disgust is an emotion meant to protect us from contamination, or signal to us a violation of our rights. Was my disgust warning me against a deep inner violation that was caused by staying in the relationship? Did I feel like my relationship was contaminating my sense of Self?

My emotions were trying to tell me it was time to "declutter" and let go, but I didn't listen.

Oddly enough, at that time in my life I *truly believed* that most people detested their romantic relationships and (if they were honest enough) themselves as much as I did. And still, being with my partner seemed less painful than being without him. Without a relationship, I had no idea who I was, and it felt like my entire existence was being threatened by the mere thought of the partnership ending. Now I understand that the opposite was true; staying in my marriage was existentially threatening.

I had to come to terms with the fact that I had married the wrong person, and accept the fact that this one mistake might define me. I had to get over my fear of ending things—the fear of being labeled a twenty-four-year-old divorcée, the fear of being left with just myself, whom I would have to sit with and listen to and give space to in order to redefine. I had to get rid of the thing that most threatened me existentially—my marriage—and provide space for my Self to act, to move, to grow, and to realize my potential. And that's exactly what I did.

Decluttering relationships is possibly the most difficult challenge of all. In our relationships, we often invest a lot of time, energy, and sense of worth. We also often hold assumptions and beliefs that prevent us from walking away,* such as:

- "No relationship is perfect."
- "They would be crushed without me."
- "I don't want to end up alone."
- "I gave them my word."
- "My family will react poorly."
- "I'm being selfish."
- "No one will want to date me."

---

* Assumptions become a problem when we don't contextualize them.

I am not going to repeat, again, just how important our relationships are . . . *but our existence does depend on them.* Most of us are scared to evaluate our relationships (romantic or otherwise), but here are several questions that can make the process easier:

- Which relationships are built on fear, guilt, or obligation?
- Which relationships have an inaccurate understanding of who you are?
- In which relationships can you show up as your Self?
- Which relationships nurture who you want to become?
- Which relationships are built on trust and honesty?

There is sometimes too much emphasis placed on when, how, and why to cut people out of our lives, and I believe it's important to acknowledge the types of people worth keeping close:

- People who tell us the truth
- People who encourage us
- People who model qualities we admire
- People who call us out (lovingly and respectfully)
- People who are willing to see us for who we are
- People who accept us
- People who respect us
- People who want what's best for us

Mistakes and Wounds

Have you ever made a mistake and then wholly embraced that one misstep as your identity? I see this in my practice all the time. If we were hurt by someone, we become a *victim*. If we cheat, we become a *cheater*. If we drop out of school, we become a *dropout*. If we get a divorce, we become a *divorcée*. But, we don't actually *become* any of these things; they just become a part of us. As a consequence, we are met with the tasks of healing, reconciling, or forgiving ourselves.

We can get so *lost* in the labels that we allow our past to define us and dictate future decisions rather than inform us. For example, the phrase "once a cheater, always a cheater" has stripped individuals of who they are outside of their mistake. We may as well be waving a banner in front of them that says: I DON'T BELIEVE YOU ARE CAPABLE OF CHANGE! Instead, why not refer to someone who has cheated as a person who has made a mistake? Why not approach them in a way that promotes empowerment and resilience (even if the person we are approaching is our Self)?

Similarly, I see people existing as walking billboards of their *wounds*—and why wouldn't they, when we treat them as such? It's normal to grapple with the imposition our wounds present, and feel shattered even from a single fracture. But we have the responsibility and the freedom to define our Selves, meaning we have the responsibility and freedom to do what is necessary in order for our setbacks or traumas not to consume our sense of Self. This may come off as harsh, but it's not meant to. It's incredibly unfair that after we've been hurt by someone, it's on us to pick up the pieces. However, if we don't, *we* are the only one that suffers. Identifying as solely a *victim*, although an accurate representation of what has happened to us, can rob us of our empowerment to become so much more.

Our wounds, just like our faults, are real. We are not meant to deny them, but we are meant to recognize them as just a *part* (and not the whole) of who we are. We need to stop using our mistakes as a way to overshadow or impose on our sense of identity. Most of our mistakes occur *because* we don't know who we are, not because they highlight who we are. If anything, they highlight how self-loss has manifested itself in our lives.

Letting go is not about pretending something painful never happened, belittling how it's impacted us, or acting like it didn't matter. Releasing our Self from our wounds implies changing the relationship we have to pain. A new relationship can be one of awareness and choice (all the best relationships are). It's not about ceasing to feel the pain, it's about learning from it.

We all have wounds. Some we have licked, some we are too scared to face, and others we keep picking at and deepening. Here are some questions to help you reflect on your wounds:

- What pain do you want to heal from?
- What is your relationship with your wounds?
- Are there things you struggle to forgive yourself for?
- Which wounds do you believe define you?
- How might they *inform* you instead?

Redefining your relationship to your wounds is not about toxic positivity, which can sound like:

- "Everything happens for a reason."
- "Look at the bright side."
- "It could have been worse."
- "Chin up!"

It's about understanding that wounds can create a depth that now our soul can fill. Wounds challenge and cut us, and we may not come out "stronger," but we will come out knowing what the experience is like. That can still mean something, if we let it.

Beliefs

Beliefs are a convenient place for our fears to hide. We all have beliefs, some of which we are aware of, and some of which we are not. What we believe about the universe, other people (cultures, ages, race, professions), the concepts of "good" or "bad," and anything and everything else, serves as parameters of our existence—it's how we understand the world. Being aware of our beliefs is key, especially beliefs that promote self-loss.

- What beliefs make you feel bad about your Self, and where, and/or from whom, did you acquire these beliefs?
- What beliefs do you have about others?
- What beliefs do you have about the world?
- What beliefs do you have about your purpose/meaning in life?
- How are the beliefs you listed impacting you?
- What do you believe you deserve?
- Who do you believe your Self to be?

Our beliefs also create our assumptions. Assumptions replace deliberate engagement and are shortcuts for our mind. They help us make sense of the world without having to process information all the time. However, assumptions don't leave much space for us to authentically encounter our Self or others around us.

Here are four reasons why making assumptions can be detrimental:

1. **Assumptions are often wrong.** Assumptions usually tell us more about who *we* are than who someone else is. Assumptions often reflect our fear, insecurity, bias, or prejudice.

2. **Assumptions can hinder connection.** Assumptions can prevent us from seeing and engaging with people for who they really are.

3. **Assumptions are sometimes lazy.** Making assumptions discourages us from putting in the effort to find the answers we need.

4. **Assumptions help us avoid responsibility.** Assumptions can be a convenient way to avoid responsibility, because they often lead us to place blame on others (e.g., "I treated them with disrespect because they are X"). Assumptions allow us to create a narrative that we need in order to cope with a certain situation or to justify our own shortcomings and behaviors.

I often think about space as a stage for our existence. If the stage is occupied with people and things that do not belong there, we cannot express our Self; we don't have room to play the part (*be* the person) that most aligns with us. Heidegger said, "How should the new day arrive, if the night is withheld from it and everything is suppressed into the twilight of decisionlessness?" Let's reword that: *How are we meant to be our Self if the way we exist still expresses versions that are not us?*

In the process of decluttering, I let go of many versions of myself that were created passively, submissively, and almost accidentally. And yet, although Heidegger suggested that faulty interpretations of ourselves are a stubborn obstacle to authenticity, he also argued that they are necessary:

> These faulty interpretations of transcendence, of the basic relationship of Dasein to beings and to itself, are no mere defects of thought or acumen. They have their reason and their necessity in the Dasein's own historical existence. In the end, these faulty interpretations must be made, so that the Dasein may reach the path to the true phenomena by correcting them.

I want you to know that it's okay to grapple with your sense of Self, and it's okay to stumble upon misunderstandings along the way. Trusting that it's all part of the process can alleviate some of the pressure and help us embrace being human.

The beauty is in the decision to act—to be—*now*.

So, what do you need to declutter in order to make space for your Self?

Hard Truth

Sometimes, in order to embrace who *we are*,
we need to shed everything we are not.

Gentle Reminder

Dear Self,
Lighten your load.

CHAPTER 8

The Body Electric

Reconnect and Communicate with Your Body

I always liked the saying "You can't have your cake and eat it, too." For example, you can't enjoy the freedom that comes from abdicating responsibility for your body, and at the same time savor the delicious embodiment born of fully embracing your physical self. The reality is, I've *never* met a person who rejected or ignored their body and still had a close relationship with their Self. When we reject or ignore our body, we reject or ignore an important aspect of our Self—and in order to truly *be* our Self, we must have a relationship with *all* aspects of who we are.

However, many of us know how challenging it is to build a healthy relationship with our body—and the reasons as to why we struggle feel endless. One of the more heartbreakingly common reasons—or at least the one that's talked about the most—is the unrealistic expectations set by diet trends, social media, advertising companies, the entertainment industry, various cultural norms, and sometimes even our own families. But if we stopped there, this list wouldn't include those who have been taught to ignore their bodies, those who never felt at home in their bodies, those who have learned to use their bodies to earn love or acceptance, those who've experienced physical or sexual abuse, those suffering from chronic pain or disordered eating, and those with disabilities. And lastly, I want to make sure we acknowledge those who are disappointed or feel let down by their bodies because they are unable to have a child, enjoy sex, or are losing a battle to an illness. Regardless of the specific reason(s) for not having a healthy relationship with our body, it often leads to three outcomes (or a combination of them):

1. We become disconnected from our body.
2. We become preoccupied with our body.
3. We become scared of our body.

Despite this prevalent reality, very few of us acknowledge our relationship with our body or decide to do anything about it (and perhaps wouldn't know where to begin even if we wanted to). We tend to offer our body genuine attention only when we are in pain, when it's not doing something we want it to do, or as a means of expressing dissatisfaction with the way it looks. Over time, our body becomes something we try to control and change, rather than something we enjoy, experience, and learn from.

Most of us don't bother to offer our body positive attention because we feel *entitled* to its collaboration, function, beauty, and service. Why would we validate or praise it for something we believe it "should" be doing in the first place? It's the same argument I hear when people say: "Why should I be grateful to the waiter for being nice and getting my order right? It's their job!" Yikes.

Ultimately, this privileged position in regard to our body can lead to self-loss. When we treat our body as an object, servant, or property, we don't bother to build a relationship with it—nor, consequently, with our Self. You might be a little shocked by this attitude, but unfortunately it's very common.

This way of thinking about our body is often rooted in believing that the mind and body are separable or at war with each other (also known as dualism). This framework is often accompanied by various assumptions. One is that there is a hierarchy of importance (mind over body) or that the mind is "virtuous and good" and the body is "sinful and bad." This particular assumption can be harmful, because we've been subjected to beliefs that perceive our body as a hindrance to self-actualization, urging us to "transcend it." Such narratives have created a disconnect and, for some, even self-estrangement. We have unknowingly robbed our body of its meaning and power.

Listen: *There is no hierarchy when it comes to the Self; no aspects that take precedence over others.* The Self is about cohesion and alignment. Acute awareness in one regard does not compensate for blissful ignorance in another. Being aware of our detrimental cognitive or emotional patterns does not offset our lack of connection with our body.

So, then, why do we believe that who we really are is something "more" or "better" or "wiser" than our body?

Part of the answer is that we have reduced the body to its

biological functions and physical properties (e.g., appearances). We have begun to see it merely as a tool, and not an entity that is present, feeling, sensing, and communicating—and in doing so, we have characterized the body as something different, separate from who we are. This disconnect, or objectification, has changed the way we view our body. Instead of understanding it as a major part of who we *are* (a reality we must learn to accept), we now see our body as something external (a project in need of constant alteration or modification). Our body has become something we can reject or discard. Some of us might even see it as something foreign, something that's not even a part of us. As a result, it has ceased to be a safe "space" for many of us; instead, it has become a social currency with which we buy love, acceptance, and our place in this world.

The value of our body is often sought in what it gives us, rather than in what it *is*. And, of course, there is value in what the body offers, but our body holds inherent worth and purpose without which we do not exist. *Let's take a moment to allow that to soak in.* Society frequently talks about self-love, body-positivity, or body-neutrality as a way to encourage a healthy mindset and nurture self-acceptance. Although admirable movements, they miss an important link that makes the goal—a genuine understanding of our bodies, and of the connection between our bodies and our sense of Self—nearly impossible. To me, these approaches are a little like trying to do an open-heart surgery with a first aid kit.

In order to change our relationship with our body, we must first understand what the body is.

EXISTENTIAL UNDERSTANDING OF THE BODY

Not long ago, I asked my Instagram community a simple question: "When do you feel most like your Self?" I received an overwhelming amount of responses, and despite there being thousands of varying answers, there was one common theme: *embodiment*. Most of the responses listed activities—hiking, dancing, stretching, deep breathing, crying, sex—that allowed them to engage and experience their body. It's in those moments of embodiment that they felt most authentic, alive, and aligned. Why were the answers not "when I read a magazine" or "when I watch Netflix"?

Because embodiment is a way of creating authenticity.

Our sense of personal agency, cohesion, and continuity in time is based on embodiment—which means that if we remove the body, we remove our access to the Self, and, arguably, the sense of Self itself. As humans, we experience the world through our bodies, perceiving and interacting with the things around us to the degree to which our bodies allow or constrain. *Life enters through our bodies;* the body is power.

Maurice Merleau-Ponty—a French philosopher best known for his contributions to phenomenology—writes that "the body is our general medium for having a world," and later, "Inside and outside are inseparable. The world is wholly inside and I am wholly outside myself." In a nutshell? *By experiencing our body we are able to experience and know our Self.* Without experiencing the world through our body, there is no Self. It's not surprising, then, that the Self is not "found" within our minds, but in our "*corps vivant*"* (lived body). The lived body allows us to experience, participate in, and grasp life.

Existentially speaking, as humans, we not only "have" a body, but we—even more significantly—*are* our body (for our Self and for others). A body is more than flesh and a beating heart (more than what we see in the mirror). Although one aspect of our body *is* characterized by the body's faculties—objective abilities, limitations, properties—the body is more than a biological output or a *tool* used by our spirit. I understand Heidegger's concept of *Dasein* (being-in-the-world) as a dynamic between the subjective Self (mind) and objective Self (body) in which they mutually comprise and shape each other. This occurs when our body participates with its lived experiences, and preserves closeness with its sensations and feelings. It's these body sensations that represent *being alive; existing*.

Body-Subject and Body-Object

When someone glances at us, it reveals our presence and confirms that we exist. This is why when someone refuses to look us in the eye—or to look at us at all—our instinct might be to go: "Hey! I am right here! See me!" We *want* our existence to be confirmed, recognized, and perceived—and we can only be perceived because we have a body. Yet the body doesn't merely represent itself, it represents who we *are*. Simply put, our body is like our mediator, an agent that is in the world.

* A popular term used by Merleau-Ponty.

My boy Jean-Paul Sartre wrote and talked extensively about the objective and subjective experience of one's Self. Generally, we experience our Self as the subject (the narrator of the story), but if someone stares at us long enough, we can become aware that we are an object in *their* subjective experience (*their* story). As human beings, we are asked to simultaneously hold these two realities in our mind: that we are all agents—the main characters of our own lives—but we are also supporting characters in *other people's* lives: objects that others observe. (You didn't expect this to be simple, did you?)

A famous example Sartre offers is a person observing what is happening behind a closed door through a keyhole. Suddenly, they hear footsteps coming from behind. In this moment the individual becomes conscious that they have gone from being the observer to being observed. The act of being observed makes them aware that they have become an object to someone else. It's not that the observer has suddenly "objectified" us; it's what we did to ourselves when we became aware of feeling watched.

Do you know the feeling? It's that moment you are on a subway and you crane your neck to see what the stranger next to you is reading and then, suddenly, they make eye contact and shift away. Or when you are in your car jamming out to your favorite song and suddenly notice that the driver next to you is watching. In both scenarios you might feel embarrassed because, well, let's face it, being perceived can be *uncomfortable*. Our freedom feels threatened when we switch from being-for-itself (*l'être-pour-soi*) to being-for-others (*l'être-pour-autrui*); meaning, switching from my own perceived attributes (how I understand my Self to be) to having attributes ascribed to me based on who I am for someone else.

Likewise, in our own perceptions and narratives about other people (the objects), it's important to remember that we don't actually gain knowledge *about* the other—not *really*. Instead, we gain knowledge *of* the other, which allows us to experience our Self. We get an idea of how this person presents to us and how we experience them—which ultimately gives us more information about who *we* are rather than about who they are.

What I want you to remember is that who we are is determined by how we show up and experience the world. And yet, *we cannot show up or do anything in the world—we cannot exist—without our physical body*. Our relationship with our body and our body's relationship to others is complex and intertwined. It allows us to discover what makes us unique and what it means to "be our Self." If we feel unplugged or disconnected from our body, we lose our source of vitality. **We lose our sense of Self.**

Disconnection

Many of us have been taught to disconnect from our body. In our society, it's become normal to spend hours streaming or scrolling to the point that we become unaware of our physical presence. Many choose to do so because it not only releases dopamine (the "feel-good" chemical in our brains), but it also allows us to genuinely disconnect from our existence. It's almost like a part of us disappears when we are mindlessly engaging with technology.

This sense of "disappearing" happens when our body is reduced to the status of a simple object—a machine. It pumps blood, breathes air, responds to stimuli, but it ceases to be the source of our understanding of our relationship with others and our Self. This is what it means to be disconnected.

For some, this disconnect happens over time, as a consequence of something that's been taught or modeled. For others, it can occur as a result of unpleasant or painful experiences (such as a family member passing away), or a traumatic event (such as a car accident). The tricky thing about being unplugged from our physical form is that we are often unaware of it. Whenever I see a new client, I am always curious about their self-body relationship. I usually observe how they speak about their body, how they treat it, and how connected they are to their body as an entity rather than an object. I am looking out for reductionist interpretations of their body, and often I will ask if their body has anything to add to our sessions. *If your body could speak, what would it say? What is your body communicating right now?*

Misha was a twenty-four-year-old whose whole world revolved around her relationship. She signed up for therapy just so she could unpack her relationship and get tips on "how to make it work." She was very self-aware, emotionally attuned, and yet I sat there feeling like we were not encountering the whole truth. I felt like no matter how much I turned toward her, I was not seeing *her*. I didn't think that Misha was deliberately hiding anything from me; I just believed she didn't have full access to herself.

Over the years, I've learned that when our minds don't have the answers, our body usually does. So, during a natural pause in the conversation, I asked Misha to close her eyes and take deep, even breaths while thinking about her partner for sixty seconds. I started the timer, and it only took a couple of seconds for the tears to come. Eventually the tears turned into uncontrollable sobs. Once the sixty seconds were up, Misha opened her eyes wide with disbelief. She realized, for the first time, that she was scared of her partner. Her body knew something she didn't, it had held on to things she had tried to forget. We had our answer: She was struggling to navigate the relationship because she didn't feel safe being in it.

When we do not consult or listen to our body, we are more likely to ignore our experiences, therefore making it harder to recognize what we really need and to make the changes that align. We need to get used to allowing our body a seat at the table and embrace that its presence enhances our (subjective) understanding rather than limits it. This was an important lesson for Misha that day.

I see the disconnect between the Self and the body all the time. And I am never surprised. The messaging that nurtures such a dynamic is subtle and chronic. Most of us are not even aware of the fact that we have been taught to ignore, distrust, or push our body beyond its limits. Here are some phrases we may have heard that have contributed to our disjointed relationship:

- "Don't cry" (even when you're sad).
- "You can't go to the bathroom" (ignore your body's messaging until class is over).
- "Eat everything on your plate" (even if you're full).
- "Stop eating so you can stay 'thin'" (even if you're hungry).

- "Don't complain" (even when you are in pain).
- "Your body needs to be perfect" (it's okay to criticize and do whatever it takes to "fix it").
- "Your body is for others" (you don't need to build a relationship with it, just *use* it).
- "Push harder" (so others can see results).
- "You'll rest when you're dead" (ignore your body's needs).
- "Don't make a big deal about it" (numb or disregard your discomfort).
- "Don't sleep around" (tame your sexual needs or expression).
- "Don't be so dramatic" (don't express yourself in ways others won't like).

This body-self disconnect can manifest in many, and sometimes very unexpected, ways. One of my first clients was a male in his late twenties who had come to therapy to explore his pornography and masturbation habits. He noticed how his behavior impacted his dating life and was worried that he would never be able to be happy in a long-term relationship. In a span of several sessions, he expressed his frustration that no amount of logical reasoning or "self-control" had stopped him from turning on his computer and masturbating five to eight times a day. He shared that he was disgusted with himself for constantly objectifying women, and acknowledged how degrading it was. Even in this session, I could see that cognitively he was aware, but he was still disconnected from everything he was saying. There was no emotion, and only a blank expression on his face. It was as if he were reading a script someone else wrote. His frustration eventually turned into anger, and his anger turned into hopelessness.

After several weeks of working with him—listening to his narrative and normalizing his experience—I began to notice the particular language he used when he spoke about his body. He was crude, self-deprecating, and detached while describing his genitals and his desires. Initially, this was easy to miss because of the graphic way he spoke about other people's bodies.

Over time, I worked to change the conversation. Instead of talking about his relationship to other people's bodies, we began to discuss his relationship with his own body. It didn't take long for him to come to the conclusion that he was not seeking sexual satisfaction, but rather a connection with his Self. He found masturbation a grounding and embodying experience that helped him feel more present. He soon realized that this habit had begun right after a traumatic event (which he hadn't initially perceived as traumatic). Quickly after this realization, his frustration turned into compassion, and his awareness into behavioral change.

This client's journey is imprinted in my memory. Not because he was my first male client, or because it was my first time tackling the topic of masturbation, but because he taught me two important things: 1) We all seek a connection with our Self, even if we are not fully aware of the disconnect, and 2) We all have a narrative about our body (this client thought he was "out of control" and "bad"), and unless we pay attention to it, it will shape our relationship with our Self without our consent.

THE BODY NARRATIVES

Imagine a woman walking down the street at midnight. Mascara is running down her face, and she is holding her heels in her hands as her bare feet navigate the paved streets of New York. She seems intoxicated, her hair and dress disheveled. She bumps into you because she is looking down at her phone, and when you turn around to spot the person who has violated your physical space, she doesn't even bother to apologize, but just keeps going.

Most of us would feel a pang of annoyance. It would be easy to make assumptions based on the time of day, her appearance, and her demeanor. Many would jump to unkind conclusions. What people would struggle to offer—and what would be impossible for them to offer—is compassion for her specific experience (because they don't know what it is).

But . . .

What if you knew that she was married and had just caught her husband cheating? She confronted them. He got aggressive, grabbed her by her hair, and shoved her against the wall. She was scared and distraught, and so she ran out of the house with her shoes in her hand, texting her best friend to come pick her up.

What if you knew that this woman was at a bar for her friend's birthday party and got an unexpected call that her dad was in the ICU? Intoxicated, she immediately left the bar and took off her heels so she could quickly walk toward a cab that would take her to the hospital.

What if you knew that she was at a club, got drunk, hit on someone else's girlfriend, and got into a public altercation?

She didn't back down and continued to yell, making crude comments about the couple until she was asked to leave by the bouncers.

What if you knew this woman—what if, after she bumped into you, you realized that she was a cousin, a friend, a colleague?

What if you recognized your Self in her?

Did each of these narratives change the way you felt about the person in this story? Of course it did. The more details we know, the more our relationship to something changes.

It's hard to love, or even like, someone we don't know very well. It's hard to recognize someone's true value when we are separated by distance or missing information. It's hard to build a genuine connection with those we do not communicate with. When we encounter strangers (those unfamiliar to us), it's easy to judge, be scared, or make assumptions. It's easy to use strangers as a blank canvas for our own projections, assumptions, biases, and insecurities.

If our body is someone we do not know—a stranger—we do these same things to it. And, consequently, we deepen our self-estrangement. But the more we know—the more we are aware—the more likely we are to build a narrative that is grounded in reality. It will force us to reconcile what we think about who we are and how we experience our Self.

It's only when we are willing to turn toward and understand our body (to one degree or another) that we become open to intimacy, respect, and compassion. This is the premise that informs my clinical work when helping clients reconcile their body-self relationships. *If we struggle with our body, we are most likely missing the understanding that would off-*

set any judgment, fear, or criticism. To understand the Self, we need to embrace, and be *willing* to embrace, all that the body contains—wisdom, depth, and the elements that make up our essence.

The narrative of our body is sometimes restricted by how we "want" to see it, and what relationship with it we believe would be beneficial to maintain. It's tempting to say, "I don't like my body" instead of "I don't like my Self." It feels safer. I've noted in my work that many people project their insecurities and disappointments onto their body. Instead of facing the hard truth that they struggle to build connections, they will gladly blame their body for being dumped ("It must have been because of the way I look"—not because they were rude to the waitress, or because they lacked things in common, or because they wanted different things from the relationship). In some instances—not all—our body has become the scapegoat in the story of our Selves.

Do you understand the story of your body?
What narrative and beliefs shape your perception of it?

Start by defining the word "body" for yourself. The following are some prompts that can help get you started. Depending on your life experiences or your "givens," these questions may feel harder to answer than they might be for others. But regardless of who you are, the exploration of your body remains important.

- What does your body mean to you?
- How would you describe your relationship with it?

- How do you want your relationship with it to change?
- What events have impacted your relationship with your body?
- How has your body helped you? How has it hurt you?
- What did your caregivers/relationships teach you about your body?
- Do you feel like your body is an asset, or something you are insecure about?
- How do you want to refer to your body: *it, her, he, they, self,* etc.?
- What emotional wounds need to be healed in relation to your body?
- What do you expect from your body?
- Does your body feel like *you*?
- When do you feel most connected to it?
- What part of you do you think your body misrepresents or ignores?

The process of changing our relationship with our body begins with evaluating and rewriting the narratives and beliefs we currently hold about it. In an effort to help you start this process, I'll explore some common narratives that people have about the body, which can help you start thinking about your own relationship to yours.

Narrative #1: My Body Is Not a Safe Space

One of the most prevalent narratives for many of us is that our body is not a safe space. We may be hesitant to trust or appreciate our body if we feel like it's working against us (e.g., when we have anxiety attacks). We may also feel threatened by its natural aging process—inducing worry that our "value" is depreciating. As human beings, we are scared of the unfamiliar and the things we cannot control. And, to our dismay, our bodies are undergoing constant changes (shape, weight, height, hair color, skin texture, bone-withering). This is why the relationship we have with our body is complex and always in flux. The truth is, our bodies wear, tear, decay, and eventually expire. We have been conditioned to be dissatisfied with, or even ashamed of, our bodies changing (e.g., we are often unhappy about our body doing exactly what it's meant to do), and instead of celebrating the longevity (if we're lucky!) of our relationship with it, we become progressively dissatisfied. Moreover, we've been socially "justified" in our cruelty and have been rewarded for every attempt to enhance, change, or "perfect" the way our body looks. No wonder it doesn't feel like a safe space! No wonder that, for many of us, it's portrayed as the villain of our story. We've *got* to change this narrative, and in order to do so, we need to trust our body's process and wisdom.

I know what it's like to feel that my body is not a safe place. Like many, I've taken turns feeling disconnected, consumed, and frightened by it (all to varying degrees).

Fear wasn't the first point of contention I had with my body, but it was by far the most consuming. In my early twenties, I was terrified of my panic attacks. I perceived my body as temperamental and irrational; without any warning, she could paralyze me. But this seed of fear of my body was actually planted in high school—during an odd phone call.

One morning when I was sixteen, I was home alone and getting ready for school when a man called to conduct a "survey."

I was caught by surprise and had that familiar tinge of dread that came every time I accidentally picked up such a call. He began by asking how old I was, and I immediately told him I was underage. A normal survey would have ended with this piece of information, but as I was about to hang up, he caught me by surprise by saying, "That's okay." That should have been my sign to hang up, but I was confused, so I stayed on the line.

He started with innocuous enough questions—what music did I listen to, what TV shows did I watch, what brands and colors did I like to wear? Then he asked for more personal information about my age, height, hair color, and what high school I attended.

The alarm bells in my head started to ring. So, I lied. And every time I did, he laughed or uttered "mm-hmm" in a way that let me know he didn't believe me. Then he asked, "What is your bra size?"

I went silent. My heart began to pound in my ears. After a few seconds he said, "Hello?" I snapped out of my shock and slammed the phone down.

I checked the caller ID. It was a blocked number.

Maybe it was a prank call, maybe it wasn't. Regardless, it felt threatening. Given the nature of the questions the man asked me and the sequence of events that followed—more un-traceable phone calls, strangers parked or standing in front of our building—the police believed I may have been the target of a human trafficking attempt. There was a supposition that because I walked to school by the same route every day, per-haps they had been following me for a while and knew what I looked like. I felt threatened, and the first thing I blamed was my body. From then on, I often thought, *If I didn't look the way I looked, I wouldn't be in danger. If my body wasn't de-sirable, maybe people wouldn't want to use it or hurt me.*

Fast-forward a couple of months to the start of my fresh-man year of university. Within weeks, I had a stalker (I'm serious; like, a *kill-your-boyfriend-and-lock-you-in-a-basement-*type stalker). He believed he heard God talking to him and was convinced that he was the new Adam and I was his Eve. In his mind, we were meant to repopulate the world and share the "good" message. Whenever I looked around, he seemed to be there—watching from a distance. He followed me every-where, and not subtly; it was almost like he felt it was his *right* to oversee my life. I felt threatened (again), and the people in my life got progressively more uncomfortable being around me, the walking target. He was perceived as relatively danger-ous by campus security, and was eventually hospitalized for mental health–related struggles. I was not physically harmed (lucky again), but my fear-based narrative about my body so-lidified.

If I dress up or show skin—will I be in danger? Is the way I look a threat to my life? Is it safe to show up in the world? I couldn't leave the house without going through these ques-tions. It took almost ten years for these fearful thoughts to subside and for me to rewrite the narrative. In the meantime, I always walked with keys in my hand, wore limited makeup, and never showed too much skin. I know I am not the only woman who's struggled with this narrative.

Narrative #2: Our Body Is a Project

Our body has been stripped of its depth and purpose, leaving it bare and vulnerable to societal demands. Our very happiness can sometimes feel like it hinges on the way we look—with the culture's ideal shape changing every couple of years. I grew up watching countless movies that promoted the trope of a dorky girl undergoing a music-accompanied makeover before she finds the love of her life. But even the pretty and popular girls were dissatisfied. You've all seen *Mean Girls*, right? You know the scene in which the three girls stand in front of the mirror and identify the things they hate about their bodies: hips, calves, shoulders, weird hairlines, big pores, and nail beds? The main character—played by Lindsay Lohan—seems shocked by the fact that there are so many things that can be "wrong" with someone's body. And this is where the truth comes out: There is no body or makeover that will be "enough" for society, because the standards are fickle and unrealistic. We are all encouraged to look like women on social media or in movies, even though they themselves don't even look like their pictures, and many of them don't like the way they look.

Many of us, for one reason or another, have accepted the challenge of earning our worth through our appearance. I've worked with many clients who took the project *very* seriously and jeopardized something significant (their Self) for something unattainable (perfection).

Ester battled with her body-self relationship for as long as she could remember. It was equally upsetting and unsurprising that she grew up hearing a stream of relentless criticism from her mother. As early as pre-puberty, she was told that she was "fat" and was forced to diet. She grew up lacking confidence, struggling with her relationships with others (particularly men) and her relationship with her Self. Her self-talk was beyond unkind; it was vicious. She had a deep-rooted belief that if she were to look different, all her problems would be solved—she would love her Self, men would want to date her, and she would earn her family's approval.

So, she undertook dangerous and restrictive diets and underwent five elective cosmetic surgeries. At first, they were surgeries she felt she "needed"—liposuction, and getting rid of extra skin post weight loss. But then she began to make more and more "tweaks," like breast augmentation. She'd temporarily feel better, until she didn't. After her final round of plastic surgery, which involved an excruciatingly painful recovery, it suddenly dawned on Ester that the way she looked would never solve her problems (or change the way she felt). She mourned the suffering and the risk she had put her body through. She had altered her body and now looked "wonderful" by mainstream standards, and yet she still struggled to love and accept her Self. She still wasn't happy about who she was. No amount of physical alterations could quiet her insecurity, shame, and anxiety about not being "good enough" or "worthy" of love. She couldn't recognize the value of who she *was,* and losing weight and changing the shape of her nose didn't solve the problem.*

In a society that is obsessed with self-image, it's easy to allow the way we look to devalue, or degrade, our bodies. But focusing only on our body's appearance would be like admiring the world's best heart surgeon for their hair. If we *only*

---

* I am by no means advocating against plastic surgery, but I believe that the intent, reason, and feelings that drive the decision will shape the experience and the impact it has on one's life.

care about what our body *looks* like, we are robbing our Self of our whole identity, and our sense of purpose.

Narrative #3: Our Body Is a Tool

Trisha was in her late twenties when she found herself in one of the longest relationships she had ever been in—fifteen months and counting, with a baby on the way. One day, she came into our session feeling heightened anxiety about the state of her sex life. She was worried that the frequency of sex in her relationship was decreasing (as she was becoming more physically uncomfortable during her pregnancy), and that her partner was going to leave her because of it. Although she understood that she had many appealing traits, she still didn't think they would be enough to keep him if he was not sexually satisfied. She enjoyed having sex with him, but admitted that she felt the primary function of having sex was to ensure that *he* was happy. This idea was not new for her. She had used her body in order to please, belong, and receive acceptance ever since she was a preteen, when she would make out with boys at parties so she could keep getting invited. And it always ended the same way, with her feeling used and empty. That's because our bodies are not tools that we can loan out to others; they are an integral part of who we are. Trisha was unaware of how much she was sacrificing, because she was unaware of how much her body was worth.

This is not to say that we cannot accomplish goals in collaboration with our body—like run a marathon, dance in our living room, or masturbate. It's when we use our body like currency, or for a transaction, that we undercut its value. It's when we detach our Self from *experiencing* the body in order to use it. It's when we lose sight of how sacred our body is and the significance of what it represents.

> *Have you ever used your body in a way that didn't align with who you are?*
>
> *Have you ever acted in a way that didn't resonate (didn't feel "right")?*
>
> *Have you ever thought of your body as a tool rather than an extension of your Self?*
>
> *Have you ever lost sight of the fact that your body is your source of life?*

Narrative #4: Our Body Is for Others

Most of us deem our body valuable only when other people do. We form a narrative about our body by reflecting on how others have treated us. One of my clients, Olivia, was a successful and intelligent woman in her early forties who was struggling to date. She not only intimidated most of her dates with her ambition and financial success, but many lost interest after they found out that she was a virgin (at least that was her interpretation of what happened). She was raised in a conservative home and, although she no longer held views that aligned with the purity culture she grew up in, she was faced with her glaring lack of sexual experience.

She defined herself as "undesirable" and "unfeminine" because her body hadn't been lusted after or explored by others in a sexual way. Little by little, she began to demean her own worth because of the lack of interest from others. Olivia spoke about not feeling "woman enough." I understood where she was coming from: If she believed that her body was meant *for* others, then others' lack of interest would lower her own appreciation of her body—of her Self.

Despite reading erotica, buying her first vibrator, facilitating an online discussion group, and starting to participate in free sex chat rooms, Olivia said she still felt "incompetent." So, she began to write erotic fiction as a way to express her desires and fantasies, and connect to her sensual self. But since her actual dates usually led "nowhere," she would come to sessions feeling discouraged as a result of being ghosted—yet again—after revealing the fact of her virginity, or because someone had made a snide remark about not wanting to be "responsible" for her first time. They wanted to "have fun," and not be her "training wheels." They also wondered about what was "wrong" with her if she was in her forties and a virgin. Eventually, she began to self-sabotage (act standoffish, make inappropriate jokes, avoid vulnerability or honesty) as a way to push people away and perpetuate this narrative that no one wanted her because she was a virgin. Deep down, she felt disappointed by her body, but also scared of trying something new. She'd attached meaning to her virginity that she was not willing to let go of just yet.

Unknowingly, Olivia had allowed other people's actions (and her own assumptions and fears) to shape one of the most important relationships she will ever have—her relationship with her body.

Have other people's actions or words impacted the way you feel about your own body? How?

RECONNECT WITH YOUR BODY, FIND OUT WHO YOU ARE

It's not easy to build or rebuild a relationship with our body, but it is possible. Once we have deconstructed our narrative, we need to reconstruct it—not just the narrative, but also the relationship. It's not enough to simply "understand" the body cognitively, we need to be able to experience it—to *embody* it. Part of doing this work is connecting, emotionally and mentally, but also physically.

Six Ways to Connect with Your Body

1. Monitor your self-talk. Start by observing how you speak to and *about* your body. If you have nothing kind to say, don't say anything at all. When someone compliments your appearance, don't dismiss it or make self-effacing jokes; *enjoy* it. If you choose to speak to your body (either through your thoughts or out loud), make sure the words are genuine. You don't need to be "positive," you just have to be respectful. Stop yourself from being cruel, and refrain from pointing out your flaws in front of others. A general rule of thumb is: If you wouldn't say it to your best friend, don't say it (or think it) to your Self. I know how hard this is; it requires discipline and practice. Don't worry if you slip. The first step is just to observe, and then try to lessen the cruelty. Over time, you'll see how kindness comes easier, and your respect for your body—and your Self—is bolstered.

2. Be curious. Allow your body to be part of the conversation. Meaning: *Listen* to it, to what it *really* wants in any

given moment. Does it need rest or fresh air? Does it *not* want to have sex right now? What is your body language or heart rate trying to communicate? Keep an open dialogue and slowly learn to build a sense of closeness and intimacy with the physical elements of who you are. Get curious about why your headaches seem to happen only when you work on specific projects, or why your anxiety flares up right before seeing your partner. Your body is wise, so hear what it has to say. Don't reduce or restrict your understanding of it. Acknowledge that your relationship with it is ongoing, and that you will have to stay alert in order to keep up with this complex and ever-changing entity.

3. Identify and fulfill your body's needs. When your body gives you clear signs that it needs to hydrate, sleep, eat, or move—stop assuming you know better or that there are no consequences to ignoring what it has to say. By fulfilling its needs, you are building self-trust and showing self-respect.

4. Move and interact with your body. Give your body the permission to move and express itself. This will help you genuinely experience what it's like to be you, as you get to know your body in a more intimate, primal, and vulnerable way. Dance, eat, make pottery, hike, swim, run, have sex. Do something that makes you feel your heartbeat, that moves you a little out of your head and into your five senses. If you're overwhelmed about where to start, I hope you find joy and freedom in experimenting. Try a bunch of activities and see what resonates—pay attention to what makes you feel like you're truly alive!

Here's what I tell my clients to do:

- Pick a song that reflects your current mood.
- Find a place where you can have privacy and space to move around.
- Light some candles, turn down the lights, open your windows for a nice breeze, or throw down a yoga mat. Do whatever will give you the calm, pleasant setting you need.
- Press play and start to move your body in a way that it wants to move. Let it guide you. This may look like stretching, dancing, jumping, head-banging, lying on the ground and slowly sitting up, conscious breathing, etc.
- Don't try to make it look pretty or have any sort of structure, and don't do it in front of a mirror. The whole point is for your body to express itself however it chooses, unselfconsciously.

When the global pandemic hit and we were all housebound, I began to do this "exercise" daily. At first it felt awkward, but soon I was too focused on the release, connection, and intimacy that came from observing, experiencing, and surrendering to my Self. The fact that I probably looked ridiculous was entirely inconsequential. I mean really, *who cares*? If I saw someone through a window dancing unabashedly, I'd only feel impressed and inspired, maybe even a little jealous.

Can you take a few minutes to try it?

Afterward, reflect for a moment. What emotions, thoughts, or even judgments came up for you? What did you notice in your body? In your chest and shoulders? In your stomach? In your forehead? How does it feel to surrender and trust? Did you find it hard to be intuitive? Keep doing it; I promise it gets easier to hear what your body has to say.

5. Scan your body. Many of us are unaware of how our body is feeling or if it's holding any tension until we are physically in pain or emotionally expressing that tension.

   Let's try something together. Close your eyes, take a couple of deep breaths, and identify any tension in your body. Where do you feel it? Now describe it to yourself. What does it feel like? Is it hot and fiery? Is it cool and tight, like a block of ice? Does it have movement? Mine often lives as constricting pressure in my jaw, or a painful tightening of my shoulders. If these tension-filled parts of your body could speak, what would they say?

   Now scan your body again. Identify the parts that feel the most relaxed, centered, and grounded. What do you notice? Where is there an absence of tension? What does it feel like? Describe the sensation. Again, if these parts of your body could speak, what would they say? Mine often say, "You're safe," "Notice the peace within your Self," or "It's going to be okay."

   This is an easy exercise that not only can help us become aware of how our body is experiencing and reacting to the world in any particular moment, but can also help us ground our Self physically in the present.

6. Breathe dynamically. Let's first start by getting you to simply notice your breath. Don't try to manipulate it. Is it

shallow? Deep? Rapid? Slow? Now I want you take a deep inhale and notice yourself come up against the limits of your lungs. Observe how you are held inside. Hold your breath until you are "forced" to exhale, and then exhale as much as possible until you are "forced" to inhale again.* The goal is to consciously experience this transition point where you are seemingly powerless but then guided by the wisdom of your body. You can feel the life force in you. You can learn to trust your Self to stay alive, to depend on your Self.

This is a good exercise to remind us that we have freedom, but within confines that we cannot change. Our body pushes us back to its limits. Even with the greatest will, the resistance is firm and immovable. Its power comes over us and asks us to surrender. This is not threatening, it's *vitalizing*. It allows us to feel the power of life and develop a more secure, centered, and grounded sense of Self.

Remember, all relationships take time and require care and consistency—it's not enough to meditate once and stretch twice. Keep in mind that your relationship with your body is one you want to nurture, not just a tool you want to use every now and then. Learn to honor your body's wisdom, allow it to be part of the conversation, and treat it as a fundamental aspect of your *Being*. Stay mindful of the fact that the body is the way through

---

* Shout-out, once again, to Längle for this simple but incredibly powerful technique!

which we experience the world and, consequently, our
Self.

As you know, when I was nine years old, I spent what felt like endless months in bomb shelters. Over time, my family members and I learned to pretend that our bodies didn't exist, as a way to suppress the needs we had but couldn't fulfill. And yet, the remarkable thing was that the only moments that preserved our sense of humanity, and arguably our dignity, were the ones in which we expressed our Selves through song and dance. It was in those rare instances that we displayed the things we were too frightened to say and leaned into the hope we were too cautious to have. And it was in these embodied moments that I found small but treasured glimpses into my sense of Self.

When we are treated by the world as nothing, when our life is threatened or perceived as trivial, this is when we *need* to feel our Self, to prove that we exist. This is an active process; an act of rebellion. If our relationship with our body is passive, then it will hold the qualities of any passive relationship— lacking attunement, commitment, follow-through, and joy. Unless we recognize the value, significance, and power of our body and choose to treat it with respect, we are likely not going to bother to actively interact with it.

There is no Self without the body, and yet most of us have not learned how to have a relationship with it. Now it's up to us to teach ourselves—slowly, gently, patiently. We must first release the narratives that blind us, and then allow our body to deepen our understanding of who we are. We cannot see one corner of a painting and understand its full intention or grasp its entire beauty. We are the complete work of art, and our body merely the canvas—an entry point into our existence. When we slow down and pause, we can restore our presence, our vitality, and our connection with our body. Then, and *only* then, can we restore our connection with our Self.

Hard Truth

You can't reject or ignore your body and still have a close relationship with your Self.

Gentle Reminder

Your body has a lot to say. Listen.

CHAPTER 9

Feel It All

Experience and Express Your Emotions

As a society, we are not particularly comfortable with emotions—other people's or our own. It's unlikely you'll hear someone say, "Oh my god, did you see how emotional Karen got at the party last night?" and interpret it as a compliment. Or, after seeing a person scream into a pillow, most of us wouldn't think, *Yes, queen! You're killing it at life!* When someone expresses their emotions (particularly seemingly "negative" emotions), they are often mocked, judged, or thought to be acting from a space that has clouded their "better judgment." Somehow, being "emotional" has become a synonym for being "unreasonable" or "out of control." We often feel, and in return make others feel, embarrassed for simply *having* emotions.

This isn't just the case with emotions like anger or sadness; it's also with joy or excitement. Have you ever seen someone reunite with a friend, win a prize, or meet a celebrity and have a complete happiness meltdown? Did you ever think to yourself: *They need to calm down*, or *That's a bit much*. I'm certainly guilty of this.

But let's park the judgment, and talk about the fact that the reason most people can't stand to witness or feel emotions is because they don't know what to do with them. There are many basic human skills that our society, families, and educational institutions have failed to teach us: how to set boundaries, communicate, cultivate self-awareness or meaningful relationships—and how to healthily interact with and express emotions.

Worse yet, we have been taught lessons that we are now burdened with unlearning. How many of us have been told we are too much, too dramatic, or too sensitive? How many kids have been asked to lower their voice when they were excited, or got grounded for being angry? How many have been instructed to "stop crying" before the parent even knew why they were crying in the first place? Too many.

Often, children who were praised for being "mature" are those who felt they had to suppress their emotions, or take care of their caregiver's emotional needs. And it's these same children who are now adults sitting in my office, trying to learn how *not* to prioritize other people's feelings over their own, or how to stop judging and dismissing their own emotional needs.

What I've noticed in my clinical work is that clients who suffer from self-loss often grew up with caregivers who had unhealthy or contentious relationships with their own emotions. In such households, emotions were often ignored, suppressed, or worse yet, punished. Many of my clients rarely witnessed their caregivers express feelings, or if they did, it was only done in ways that were confusing, overwhelming, destructive, or hurtful. Many were discouraged to identify or express their own emotions by being faced with a constant stream of dismissal or questioning of their experience— hearing from their parents things like "Was it really *that* bad?" "I went through worse," and "What's wrong with you?" Once our emotions are rejected by our family system, we are likely to assume they will be rejected in other relationships as well. And we are more likely to reject them ourselves.

Instead of our emotions being received with validation or support, many of us were often asked to explain, justify, or defend them. Our emotional needs were rarely (if ever) truly met, and over time we learned that our feelings were pointless or unsafe, and that our expressing them was a weakness, or even a burden to others. This is why, from a very early age, many of us built a strained relationship with our feelings. We learned that they are something we shouldn't trust, something we need to hide, control, or judge. Considering that we now know that self-expression is the only way to *be* our Self, we essentially learned a lesson that made it nearly impossible to be who we are.

It's easy to feel frustrated and let down by our family structure or role models for creating generational cycles that we now must break. But chances are that, at one point, these actions and beliefs served a specific purpose (for them and for you). Regardless of whether your emotions make you feel uneasy, or you avoid them, or you struggle to manage them, if the type of relationship you have with your emotions no longer serves you, it's time to change it.

I am not going to dive into the science behind emotions (there are plenty of other books that do that); rather, I want to discuss the *philosophy* of emotionality. Ready?

I was taught that emotions are *the experience of being moved*. How beautiful is that? I would personally go a step further and say that emotions are *the inner movement of our Being*. They are not just a subjective way we feel about something, but *the pulse of our existence*.

Let's read that again. It's important for us to understand the gravity and significance of emotions, especially if we are someone who is struggling to see the point, or find purpose, in having them.

And yet, even though emotions are incredibly important, did you know that—according to Jill Bolte Taylor, a neuroscientist and author—the physiological life span of an emotion is roughly ninety seconds? More specifically, she says:

> Although there are certain limbic system (emotional) programs that can be triggered automatically, it takes less than 90 seconds for one of these programs to be triggered, surge through our body, and then be completely flushed out of our blood stream.

Shocking, isn't it? Chances are you've spent more than ninety seconds feeling angry, sad, or happy. So, why did the emotions linger? The short answer is that the narratives we tell and retell ourselves retrigger these feelings over and over again. Instead of witnessing the emotion—noticing how we feel and how it's being expressed in our body, and appropriately responding—we latch on to the *thought* that evoked it in the first place. It's the attachment, interpretation, or meaning we attribute to the thought or situation that perpetuates the feeling, and keeps us hostage.

So, at what point does how we feel become a choice? If we keep feeding or dwelling in the narrative that hurts us, is it on us? Does it mean we *choose* to feel this way? Dr. Jill answers this question by saying: "After their 90 seconds have come and gone, I have the power to consciously choose which emotional and physiological loops I want to hook into."

Phew! There is that theme of *choice* again.

This perspective is not meant to blame us for feeling hard things, but rather to empower us. It perfectly aligns with the existential notion that *emotions pass through the essence of a person*—they "transition through personal freedom."

This is why emotions are always rooted in a *reason*—meaning, we always have a "why" for feeling what we are feeling. *Reasons* communicate the things we individually and intrinsically value. And *values* are the things we perceive and feel as subjectively worthy or unworthy (and therefore they help us engage deeply with our own existence). They are what we deeply care about! And, to take it full circle, values are the underlying reason for our preferring one thing over another. We call something a value when it touches us and produces a positive feeling (or the opposite: when it produces a negative feeling or doesn't align). Experiencing how our emotions resonate with our values is how we directly participate with our emotions and, in turn, with our Self.

For instance, if you value beauty, you may feel overwhelmed by a striking painting or piece of music. If you value life and justice (as most do), seeing coverage of war on TV may produce "negative" feelings (anger, sadness), because the actions being displayed do not align with your values.

Values, most important, play a significant role in how we make decisions and exercise our freedom and responsibility. The existential task of emotions is to "detect the personally relevant values in one's experiences and stimulate one's life." Or, simply put, strong emotions mark what is important to us, thus giving those things a bigger presence in our lives.

Ask your Self: *What has evoked joy lately? What has brought me excitement? When did I last feel despair or overwhelmed?* Chances are, the answers to these questions will show you what you most value.

Bottom line: *In order to be our Self, we must feel.* This is why we are all looking to experience *something* in our lives, regardless of whether we are seeking it on a date, in our careers, or through our children. Most of us are desperate to *feel* life, but also terrified by the prospect. So we often keep our Self at arm's length. Some of us have chosen to remain lost— emotionally unavailable—because we are too scared to face what, and who, we will find inside ourselves. Others have made an unconscious habit of numbing their emotions by having a packed social calendar, religiously drinking that one glass (or bottle) of wine as soon as they get home, or depending on social media to take their minds off things.

We may not be aware of it, but *most* of us run on emotional autopilot. Most of us have not been taught or encouraged to observe, validate, or express our emotions, so it's not surprising that we don't know the person that embodies them, or that we don't enjoy living our lives.

OBSERVING EMOTIONS

We've all had those instances where our body is doing its own thing—adjusting to hormones, time zones, climates—and we notice a physiological change and then proceed to create a new story based on these feelings. For example, maybe you're on your period and the bloating plus a sad movie you watched last night got you thinking about how you will die alone, and suddenly you feel lonely and resentful (oh, have I been there!). Our narratives are powerful, *and* our narratives are not always a reflection of reality. This is why it's important to have the skill of observation, as well as the ability to separate facts from projections, assumptions, and interpretations. This will help not just our relationships with others, but also—say it with me now!—with our Self.

Observing our emotions is the first step toward understanding them. Rather than evaluating our emotions (i.e., labeling them as "good" or "bad," "positive" or "negative"), let's begin seeing them as messengers of our inner world. Let's view them as our lived experience and the essence that stems from encountering the world around us. Instead of asking, "Should I be feeling this way?" let's start wondering:

- What beliefs about emotions are preventing me from embracing them?

- What is this emotion trying to tell me about myself?
- What is this feeling trying to tell me about the way I am engaging with others?
- How have I changed as a result of this feeling?
- What value is this emotion speaking to?
- What narrative am I holding on to? Why?
- Am I feeling more than one emotion?

Our emotions provide us insight into our experiences and our Self. By feeling them in their entirety, we do not become prisoners of our emotions, we become *informed* by them. Still, it's also important to note that we do not need to sit and feel *every single thing* all the time. That would be an unreasonable expectation. It's not about being consumed by emotions, it's about being *aware* of them. It's about connecting to our Self through them.

How do we acknowledge emotions without being consumed by them?

Naturally, observing our emotions can sometimes feel overwhelming. Here is a trick I teach my clients: When you feel an especially strong emotion, try to identify one or two *other* emotions that are also present, the more the better. Although it may seem counterintuitive to try to feel *more* when you are overwhelmed, identifying multiple emotions can actually dilute the power of the consuming emotion. It will also offer a more realistic representation of what you are feeling. You may be overwhelmed, but you may also be sad, disappointed, and angry. You may feel frustrated, isolated, or simply hungry (as is often the case with me!). When trying to address our needs, we are more likely to do it well when we can specifically identify what those needs are.

In this practice, we will often find that we are experiencing contradictory emotions. But when we feel a strong emotion, most of us usually won't *allow* ourselves to feel something else that's seemingly contradictory. We struggle to hold both. A common combination, for example, is sadness and relief, yet we often ignore the relief because we don't know how to make sense of these two feelings together. So we overcommit to sadness. We may feel happy *and* scared, so we will often choose to focus on one as self-preservation (the one that makes us more uncomfortable and poses a greater threat). But we are complex human beings who can hold a vast array of contradictory emotions—each one communicating something different or representing a unique value. Until we learn to carry it all, we will only see one side of us.

How do we acknowledge that feelings are not facts?

Remember this: How we feel represents our subjective reality, and not always the facts. Just because you may *feel* rejected doesn't mean someone is rejecting you. Just because you feel insecure doesn't mean you don't have the skill to do something. Just because you are sad, it doesn't mean there is objectively a loss. This doesn't invalidate your feelings, but it does place a limitation on them. They represent your reality, your triggers, your wounds, your hormone or fatigue levels, and so much more. This doesn't mean we should dismiss feelings; it simply means that they are limited in presenting the whole, or even an accurate, picture at all times. More precisely, feelings represent how we *experience* the picture.

How do we better respond to our emotions?

We often don't notice our emotions until they overwhelm us. We have clever ways of sidestepping or ignoring our feelings so that we don't have to deal with them . . . until we do. And yet, unless we observe our emotional patterns, it's unlikely that we will change them. I've noticed that, as humans, we tend to do two things:

1. **We transform one emotion into a more acceptable one.** Example: We may transform our anger into anxiety. If we grew up in a family that was uncomfortable with anger, or if our partner becomes aggressive as a response to signs of frustration, we may have learned that anxiety is a less dangerous, or a more acceptable, emotion. Sometimes, that's self-preservation. Other times, we are allowing our lack of self-awareness to confuse the people around us. We want them to "know" why we are upset without actually telling them.

2. **We transfer frustrations.** Let's say your boss yelled at you. You understand that yelling at your boss is not an option because it would result in being fired. So you suppress your feelings and then go home and yell at your boyfriend. This is, of course, unfair. You've transferred your frustration from one person or thing to another—one who (likely) doesn't deserve it.

For example, recently I was frustrated with my friend for eating all my cereal while we were traveling. While I was telling him just how outrageous I thought his consumption of cereal was (look, I am not proud of this example) and how that box *certainly* should have lasted us a whole week during our trip, he just looked at me and said, "Tough day? I am sensing this is not about the cereal." He was right, of course. I was feeling stressed out about a disagreement with a colleague, and because I didn't know how to address it, I lashed out at him instead.

We also transfer our feelings from one issue to another. The majority of your anger may have nothing to do with the fact that someone didn't say "please" when they asked you to pass the remote, and more to do with them not considering you when accepting a job offer across the country. If you react to them not saying "please," rather than when you found out about the job, they may genuinely think you're upset because they forgot their manners. We do this when we feel like we don't have the right to be upset about something (maybe you haven't been dating for that long), so we take out our frustration in a context that feels more "appropriate."

A great way to heighten our awareness and prevent ourselves from being overwhelmed or "consumed" is to regularly check in. This can be as basic as taking a moment every day to ask: *What am I feeling? What are the emotions (plural!) that are present, and what are they communicating to me? Are there any contradictory emotions? What is my body telling me about how I feel?*

Check in with yourself before having an emotionally driven conversation. Ask: *Am I carrying something with me that doesn't belong in this current discussion?* Honesty and openness guide our self-awareness. The quicker we acknowledge a little frustration and address it, the lower the chances are that we will have a big emotional reaction to something insignificant. This also allows your brain to participate, and if your sense of reason doesn't have space, you will once again become a one-dimensional, inauthentic version of yourself.

VALIDATING EMOTIONS

It's not possible to feel all the time or to sit with feelings indefinitely. We just need to be intentional about being aware of them. Again, emotions are not good or bad, emotions just *are*. If our narrative is that certain emotions should not be felt or expressed, we may not be honest enough to really observe them. Rather, we will deny, ignore, and suppress. Many of us have been told not just to ignore the "bad" emotions such as anger, sadness, or frustration, but also to hold back our strong, "good" emotions such as excitement, joy, or awe. Many of us grew up being scolded or punished for crying, yelling, or laughing too hard and rewarded for distancing our Self from how we felt.

I am not going to pretend that we don't need external validation; as previously established in this book, we do. However, it's equally crucial that we validate our own feelings—a skill that is especially necessary for experiences we do not share with others. If we have a pain from our past that no one witnessed, we cannot use external confirmation as validation of our experience. It's nice to know people see us, but sometimes life will ask us to see our Self even when others don't.

However, it's important to understand that validating our experiences and feelings does *not* mean validating our actions. Validating our feelings can sound like:

- "I am really sad right now."
- "I am feeling overwhelmed."
- "I feel rejected even though there is no proof that it's the case."
- "That really triggered me."

It *doesn't* sound like:

- "It's okay that I did X, Y, Z."
- "People need to just get over it."
- "I've seen people do worse."

So, what happens if we don't agree with our behavior but need to validate our emotions? You can still validate your emotions even though *you* were the source of the pain. You can say, "I don't agree with my actions, but I choose to acknowledge my pain." Validation is not a stamp of approval, it's a recognition of what you are going or have gone through. For example, one can validate that they were feeling lonely and taken for granted, but they can't condone the fact that they cheated.

EXPRESSING EMOTIONS

Since childhood, I have always had a strenuous relationship with expressing my emotions. Despite being an incredibly sensitive person, I hated crying—which created more layers of feelings, because I'd become even more frustrated and angry by my emotive outbursts (talk about a vicious cycle). But by stifling my tears, I was blocking access to my Self. The one thing that always got me, regardless of whether it was in a movie plot or real life, was goodbyes. This started when I was nine years old, when I said goodbye to my dad the day I moved from Serbia to Canada following the Kosovo War. I was making this big move with my mom and siblings (my parents were already divorced). The plan was always for my dad and me to reunite, but I had no idea when I would next see him. I can still remember hugging him at the airport and feeling entirely overwhelmed by grief and uncertainty. A dozen family friends were there—as well as complete strangers—and on top of everything, I felt completely humiliated, exposed for everyone to see.

It took many, many years before I let myself cry again during a goodbye. When the floodgates finally opened, I was nineteen years old and saying goodbye to my first love. We weren't breaking up, but we were about to do years of long distance. I was devastated. I felt consumed by my sadness and utterly at a loss for what to do. I remember crawling into my uncomfortable dorm room bed, pulling the covers over my head, and asking myself:

If my tears could speak, what would they say?

They said I was scared of being abandoned; they said that my loss was deep—deeper, even, than my current experience; they highlighted my loneliness. With that in mind, instead of getting angry at myself, I understood myself, and my reaction. And it's really hard to be mean to or annoyed with someone you can truly *see* and understand.

Existentially, tears tell us that life is flowing within us; we are still here, we are alive! It's a moment we should cherish—a rare physical and biological embodiment of our inner world. This is why I try to help my clients to encounter their emotions, and therefore their Self. There is often so much judgment and criticism that prevents them from healing—and this degree of self-loathing can only exist if we lack empathy and understanding.

I had one client, Jade, who *really* resisted her emotions. She was aware of this, and characterized her life as being on "autopilot"—she did things with little intention or genuine engagement. She was honest about perceiving emotions as a threat, since—as she explained—they never "served" her. She'd been in multiple abusive relationships and, in the past, emotions had not only led her to stay in these situations, they had also been a catalyst for the violence she suffered. She started to associate her self-expression with abuse.

Jade also refused to feel as a way to preserve her self-image. She was "strong," and felt that validating her feelings would be a form of self-victimizing. She refused to be a victim. As we untangled her beliefs, Jade eventually began to change her relationship with her emotions. Soon after, she cried in a session; we were both shocked. After her tears dried, she admitted that it was the first time she had ever cried in front of *anyone*. Jade was twenty-nine years old.

Again, emotions are *never* the problem; they just *are*. However, how we *respond* to our emotions can be an issue—but not always. Crying while having a difficult conversation is *not* an issue. Smashing someone's car window because you're angry, however, *is*. Not all expression is problematic or undesirable. Some leads to deeper understanding, and some can be harmful—this distinction is important. Whatever we decide to express, we must take responsibility for. Not all emotional expression is appropriate at all times. Crying in front of my client because I had a fight with my mother, for example, would not be appropriate. It doesn't make my *emotion* inappropriate, but rather the timing, context, and outlet of expression.

Some of us are lazy; we want people to just "know" how we feel without having to tell them. It never works. *In order to be seen, you need to show your Self,* or else the other person is left to interpret and project *their* inner world onto you. And yet, not everyone *deserves* access to our emotions. It may not feel safe to be vulnerable in some situations, and forced emotional displays can be as detrimental as suppression.

To wrap it all up: Allowing our emotions to be the premise of all our decisions will often lead to inauthentic actions, but ignoring emotions will *guarantee* inauthentic actions. We need to take ownership of our emotions and decide *how* to express them, not whether or not to feel them.

So, ask yourself: Which emotion do you possess in this very moment? What do you need to do in order to truly feel and see life? How can you truly express your Self authentically and meaningfully in the world?

Answer: *Turn toward*.

TURNING TOWARD

Last November, I was in a tiny café in Amsterdam, drinking tea and writing. In the corner of the room, I saw a woman walk up to a man who was sitting down with his coffee. Once he saw her, he stood up and they embraced. At that moment they both began to cry. Instinctually, I looked away to give them privacy. A good twenty minutes later, I saw that the woman was now sitting down, still sobbing, as the man held her hand, his eyes glazed with what seemed to be grief. Suddenly, she looked at me and we made eye contact. Instead of awkwardly looking away or wiping her tears, she just held my gaze and nodded. We acknowledged the pain of life in that moment; it was beautiful. No words were needed, her tears were communicating with me. I felt like I *saw* her, like I understood her. And somehow, I too felt seen.

I was profoundly moved by her willingness to embrace her emotions so publicly. I thought she was powerful, brave. And then suddenly, accidentally even, my thinking switched as I began to ask myself: What terrible thing must have happened that would "justify" her crying publicly, and for so long? Wasn't she embarrassed? And then, *I* was embarrassed. Why would I—a therapist who encourages people to accept and express the truth of their feelings—think such a thing? What began as admiration and concern had quickly turned into an evaluation. But why? Well, if I were to be honest with myself (and you), encountering her vulnerability—even as a bystander—deeply stirred me. And for whatever reason, I was overwhelmed. Instead of honoring my feelings and cherishing this raw, real human connection, or becoming curious about what my sadness was trying to say, I disconnected by replacing attunement and connection with judgment. I was not willing to encounter my Self, so I stopped encountering her.

For a moment, I had been *turning toward* this beautiful

stranger in the café, but then—for my own personal reasons—I turned away, becoming a stranger both to her and to my Self.

Turning toward⃰ means offering genuine attention that then creates a disposition for resonance—an openness to be moved from the inside, to feel. Turning toward means starting a relationship by drawing close to a thought, a memory, a person, a piece of art, or ourselves. What makes this dynamic unique is that it requires a degree of surrender—allowing the "other" to directly affect us, allowing it to "do" something within us. The act of turning toward makes life palpable; it allows us to pay attention and be present, to experience deep connections and a sense of fulfillment. It makes us feel alive and authentic, living fully, mindfully, in each moment.

One practical way to turn toward life is to practice inner dialogue. We can start by asking our Self the following questions:

- How can I personally contribute to feeling more alive?
- What can I do to connect with life?
- What do I believe holds value for me?
- Am I allowing myself to be moved by the things I encounter?
- Am I scared to surrender? Why?

⃰ Another life-changing concept I learned in my existential analysis training. Without knowing it at the time, I was terrified of being open to, or in contact with, anything that evoked emotion in me. It was not until I stumbled upon this section in our manual that it became glaringly obvious. I realized that I was not truly existing in the world, I was numb and apathetic, always observing it and maintaining a "safe" distance (from my own life!).

- How do my "encounters" affect me?
- How does my life feel when I allow myself to experience the "other" person, place, or thing?

Turning toward anyone and anything requires a *motion*. On that autumn day in Amsterdam, I physically turned toward the woman in tears in order to *see* her—I felt deeply connected, alive, recognizing that I was in a moment saturated with meaning.

And then, quite literally, I turned away. I turned my body in the opposite direction and kept my gaze on my computer screen.

Imagine that you are turning toward a person. Your body must move and align with theirs. In order to align, we must *see* them. It's a little on the nose, right? Turning toward someone or something means we are concentrating on them, creating a space or a pathway where we can channel our attention. The space between us turns the gap into a bridge, giving both of us access to each other. We simultaneously narrow our attention to the person, while also practicing an openness to encounter what is shown. The focus of our attention is on us, on them, *and* on understanding our own emotions as we are connecting to the "other." This is our way to establish connection. Being present allows us to achieve depth in a relationship; it also allows those who are witnessing our turning toward (someone or something) to get a glimpse of our real Self.

As Längle said during my training:

Entering a relationship means letting the others be themselves. Respecting them in their existence, allowing their existence to be in my existence. Giving them room and space to be in my life.

Turning toward is also a way to offer and be offered approval, because it is a positive affirmation within itself. There is willingness and intention that is present with the motion; it's like saying, "I am ready to set myself in motion and encounter you. What's important to me is *you*!" It's a form of self-transcendence, as well as a deeper embodiment of Self. In the process of turning toward someone, we can effectively determine if the relationship is valuable, and if we want to invest our time in it.

Simply, it's assessing our inner resources—our capacity to give time, closeness, and attention. When we turn toward something painful, such as grief, we evaluate whether we are able to cope with internal or external losses.

For a long time, I didn't turn toward because I feared facing my own darkness (my own perceived nothingness). I wanted to live without submerging myself in existence. I wanted to swim without getting wet. I wanted self-awareness without the effort of self-reflection. I wanted others to *see* me authentically, even though I was still struggling—and didn't really want—to *see* myself. Turning toward is a kind of emotional connection that requires a vulnerability and a willingness to show our feelings, but it also requires the "other" to have the willingness to receive and encounter what is being shown.

And then there is **turning away**. I'm sure you can guess what that looks like. Turning away occurs when we do things that hold no value for us, things we do not like or that do not resonate with who we are (regardless of whether they are big or small decisions/actions). **Actions that don't reflect us are actions that overlook us.** It's the act of stepping over our Self, and placing more value in people and things *other* than who we are.

Turning away is an act of self-abandonment, and I would go so far as to say it's a form of self-harm. What hurts the most is the fact that we are the ones *causing* our own suffering. When we turn away, we stop being able to feel our Self, and so we effectively become strangers to our Self. Isn't it painful when others abandon, ignore, deceive, or betray us? That pain feels tenfold when we do these things to our Self.

When we do things that hold no value or inner resonance, we tend to feel drained (because we use up more energy and don't receive any in return), heavyhearted, small, insignificant, pained, restricted, empty, or even lifeless. Have you ever attended an event you didn't want to go to, been in a relationship you wanted to get out of, had conversations you weren't intentional about, or worked a job that left you feeling absolutely dead inside by the time 5:00 P.M. on Friday rolled around? You don't feel rage or sadness or joy—just depleted and apathetic.

I have. I felt *dead* in my own self-loss. There were so many things I disliked about my relationship and life at the time, but I couldn't admit any of it to myself. I was aware of my dissatisfaction and anger toward my Self, and I turned away from it so strongly that I stopped *feeling* the dislike, I only "knew" it. It's almost like seeing a funny video and thinking *lol* because you "know" it's funny, but you are not actually laughing.

My ability to intellectualize my circumstances ("Sure, I *know* I am not happy . . .") and not *feel* (". . . but I have too many things to do and can't 'waste' my time on it") made the road to change difficult and long. That's because thoughts not accompanied by feelings are more easily forgotten, overlooked, or ignored. When we allow ourselves to feel our feelings, however, our thoughts are more likely to be taken into account and addressed. This is why it often takes hitting "rock bottom" (whatever that means to you) for people to implement real change. They get to the point where it's become a visceral and existentially threatening experience that cannot be suppressed or ignored, unlike pure reason. For me, it was only after I began to have severe, physically debilitating panic attacks that I made a change.

And while feeling my feelings was painful (good lord, was it *painful*), it was meaningful, and ultimately priceless. It allowed me to get in touch with my Self in a way that no other process could. This is why emotions are critical and, in reality, the only path toward feeling what it's like to be us.

So let's stop fighting or trying to control our emotions! Trust me, the harder we try, the harder they will retaliate. And I think we all know that the truth tends to come out eventually. Our feelings are not beckoning us like sirens seducing sailors to their deaths. They are not ill-willed; they are the only way you can *be* you. Emotions are like a tide that will go in or out regardless of your permission. But instead of fighting, swimming against the current, and being tossed by the waves, allow their power and movement to buoy you, to take you *toward* your Self.

Hard Truth

The more you resist your emotions,
the more they will control you.

Gentle Reminder

If you want to know who you are,
turn toward your Self.

PART IV

The Self You Are

One thing I feel clear about is that it's important not to let your life live you. Otherwise, you end up at forty feeling you haven't really lived. What have I learned? Perhaps to live now, so that at fifty I won't look back upon my forties with regret.

—IRVIN D. YALOM

CHAPTER 10

The Art of Being Your Self

I am sitting at my desk getting ready to see my next client, when a faint knock on the door alerts me to the fact that it's 3:00 P.M. "Come in," I say.

I can hear her muffled voice even before Claire enters the room. She's talking on the phone. She pushes the door open with her elbow, her shoulder pressing the device against her ear as she holds several shopping bags in her hands. She throws a quick, distracted smile my way and walks toward her favorite spot. As she sits down in the armchair I hear her say, "Yeah, yeah, okay, yeah. I'll call you right after I am done." Then she hangs up.

Without taking a breath, she begins to tell me about her week, which includes various disagreements, errands, and annoyances. A stream of words fills the space between us as she shares every (and I mean *every*) nuanced detail of her days since we last met—from the moment she stumbled upon an old picture of her ex that caused her to emotionally spiral, to when the screen of her iPhone cracked on her way to pick up eggs at the grocery store.

Typically, I love hearing details—they help me to get the most comprehensive look at a person's life—but on this particular afternoon, I feel my Self disengaging and tuning out (therapists are people, too!).

I used to feel guilty in such moments, but then a mentor told me that if you are detached in a session, it means you're not really *seeing* the client—either you are not looking at what is being presented, or the client is concealing themselves, often through storytelling. So, since I am aware that my disconnect is a symptom of something, it is my job to address it.

I tune in, and turn toward.

". . . God, it was so *annoying* not to have him text me back . . . ugh! And you would not believe what my boss said earlier this week . . . Plus, my friend totally blew me off this weekend, which sucked . . ."

As I try to focus, I find myself getting lost again in the stream of specifics. Claire jumps around from complaint to grievance with no time to even give her words a moment to land. She is saying a lot, but appears to be experiencing very little. I can't detect emotion, awareness, or meaning in her narrative.

Is she genuinely engaging with her own life?

I am doing my best to keep track of everything. Then she says something unexpected, and I get an in: ". . . I don't even know what I want or who I am."

I sit up, alert. "Let's start there," I say, perhaps a tad too eagerly.

Although Claire and I have talked about her desire to connect with her Self—how she always had a jam-packed schedule in an effort to avoid *ever* being alone, because being by herself forced her to sit and really look at her reality (which she did not like)—she still feels overwhelmed by the prospect of facing who she is. *Who will she see? What if it's not someone she likes or respects?*

In the past, I had suggested that she practice spending more time in solitude and silence, and whenever I did, her face would crumble in genuine pain. The idea of just sitting with what was going on was, for her, agonizing. So I decide to show her how simple it can be; to demonstrate that, with a little intention and stillness, she might learn a lot about her Self. By engaging with life, as simply as with an object, she can unlock new awareness and build self-closeness. With her permission, we decide to pause on the details of what it was like cleaning her oven two days ago, and do a guided exercise.

I ask her to get comfortable in her chair. To which she responds by shifting in her seat, placing both feet next to each other on the ground, and sinking deeper into the leather. We begin by inhaling deeply together, and then I ask her to close her eyes. I repeat calming affirmations such as: "I am calm," "My mind is getting quiet," "I am comfortable and at peace with where I am in this moment." I watch her muscles relax and her eyes flutter, almost as if in a state of quiet, light slumber.

I ask, "Do you sense what you're sitting on?"

I don't need her to answer the questions out loud, but I do want her to think about them. I continue: "What does it feel like?"

After a few seconds, I ask a question that makes her eyes fly open.

"What is the chair trying to tell you?"

She looks at me, trying to figure out if I'm joking or not. I nod, and she closes her eyes, repositions herself in the chair.

"What does the chair mean to you?"

I can see her face contort into a question, and then suddenly become serious.

"What does it mean that the chair is here and you're sitting on it? . . . What is it doing *with* you? What is it doing *for* you?"

I see her breathing speed up. She's engaging with the questions.

"Can you accept what the chair is saying to you? . . . Do you like what it's saying? Are you okay with it?"

Suddenly, I see a single tear roll down Claire's face.

Softly, I continue: "What answer do you want to give the chair? What do you want to say?"

The floodgates are open. She starts sobbing, her eyes still closed.

After a minute, I shift her attention from her inner world: "Do you still sense the chair?"

She nods.

Gently, I continue: "How is the chair reacting to what you had to say?"

I let her sit with that question.

"What are you saying to each other?"

She wipes the tears that have rolled down her chin.

"Can you surrender to the chair? Happily? Freely? . . . Do you sense the trust?"

She starts to sob again. Her knees come up to her chest as her heels rest on the edge of the chair.

I give her a few moments and then ask the final questions: "Do you want to trust the chair? Do you want to surrender to it with your entire weight?"

I encourage her to remain connected to her seat until she feels okay.

Then I don't say anything. We sit in silence.

Claire continues to cry until, slowly, she plants both her feet on the ground and her breathing becomes deeper. Her tears stop.

I tell her that, when she feels like it's enough, she should open her eyes and stretch.

When her eyes open, she looks tired, but mostly shocked.

"What came up for you?" I ask.

"A lot," she says and then proceeds to tell me. Her words are calm, even-paced, and coated in thoughtfulness as she admits that feeling like this is the first time she has allowed herself to think about her body, to truly pay attention to it. How, if she is honest with herself, she feels like she never puts her whole weight on *any* chair, because she doesn't believe it can support her "frame." She then makes a connection: This is kind of like how she doesn't believe *anyone* in her life can support her. She believes that she has to bear the burden of life alone. She was "shaken" when prompted to listen to what the chair had to say—admittedly, she is not used to listening to others, instead making quick assumptions and projections, filling in the blanks with her mind. And finally, she says that having the chance to speak back to the chair—to the foundation of her life that she did not trust—felt scary, but empower-ing. She never felt like she could "talk back to life," until today.

"My mind is blown. The fact I can so quickly learn so much about my Self and genuinely learn more about the world (or in this case, the chair I am sitting on) . . . it's so simple, it's life-changing. I felt more connected to my Self than I have in years. All because of a *chair*."

I no longer feel disengaged.

That therapy session didn't unfold in this particular way merely because of the chair.* The exercise helped Claire de-velop a *phenomenological attitude*—leading her from an out-ward perception to an internalized one. A fundamental skill, in my opinion, for *being* our Self.

I know it's kind of intense to introduce a new concept toward the end of this book, but you've come this far with me (thank you!) and I promise that it's vitally important—that this is, essentially, what it all comes down to. Phenomenology comes from the Greek word *phaínomai,* which means "to ap-pear." The task of phenomenology is to gain knowledge by

---

* I remember doing a version of this exercise for the first time on an uncom-fortable plastic chair in a dark church basement during one of my existen-tial analysis trainings (it was the only space they could find to rent so last-minute, and it was beyond depressing). Professor Längle's words flowed effortlessly, and at first I couldn't stop myself from thinking how absurd it was that I was trying to communicate with my chair. I remember internally scoffing that this was some hippie-dippie shit, but that since I was paying for it, I might as well try it. Within minutes of parking my judg-ment and offering genuine attunement and attention, I was, of course, in tears.

simply *looking at* what appears and personally relating to what is perceived.* It is an attitude of gaining insight into an essence *based on what we see, not on what we know* (i.e., not on our preconceived ideas). It is a state of *openness* that takes *Every. Single. Thing. Seriously.* **It's our *devotion* to genuinely being-in-the-world.** Merleau-Ponty, in his book *Phenomenology of Perception,* said something similar:

> Nothing determines me from outside, not because nothing acts upon me, but, on the contrary, because I am from the start outside myself and open to the world.

This attitude—way of existing—is about seizing all the fleeting moments that our life comprises, moments that will never be replicated again. It's about deepening our understanding and constantly *being* our Self.

Because, ultimately, *being* (our Self) is a verb.

Längle speaks about phenomenology in terms of gaining a deeper understanding of the world by allowing it to sink in, allowing our Self to be touched, and by being open to *everything* the world shows us (a form of mindful openness). We can only do this when we look with "disarmed" eyes, without any defensiveness or motivation to use something or someone. In order for the understanding to deepen, we must go "inward" and be conscious of the impact it's having on us, and then go back "outward" to see more. We simultaneously have to grasp the impression the "other" has on us *and* how

---

* A way to practice phenomenology is through turning toward (see what I did there?).

the other person appears to us. In our impression, we capture their essence. We would never make a firm claim: "This is how you *are*!" Instead, we approach the other with the same know-ingness that we should approach our understanding of our Self: "This is how I see you now. This is how you're presenting to me as I am in this moment with you. This is what this en-counter means to me."

The observer is *part* of the observed. Keeping this idea in mind can help us make the distinction of where we end and others begin. And, most important, it can help us under-stand how the Self and the other are inextricably intercon-nected.

Everything you encounter—a chair, a painting, a glass of water, a sunset, a conversation, a stranger on the subway, yourself in the mirror after a night without sleep—is a gate-way to understanding not just your world, but your Self. Our job is to remain willing to be moved, struck, by these encoun-ters (whether they are with people, things, or ideas) and to try to understand what each instance wants to tell us.

This is the key. If you find yourself still feeling confused or overwhelmed by the prospect of becoming or being your Self, that's okay. Take a deep breath, and remember:

Your Self is at your fingertips. Look around you—that *is* who you *are*.

That day with Claire, as she connected with the chair, I connected with her. And as we both deepened our under-standing of the "other," we also deepened our sense of Self (she faced her fears, and I took responsibility for not engaging with her). It takes courage to be *in* the world—to actively engage with it moment to moment. It takes an incredible amount of courage to be your Self.

I wonder what it would be like if we all, as a society, decided to *appear* rather than conceal or recoil. What would it be like to experience our Selves rather than carry the burden of our preconceived notions and expectations? What would it be like to let others see us, and be invited to see them? What would it be like if we all actually cared to truly see one another? What would it be like if we recognized that *everything* can tell us something both about *it* and about our Self?

Recovering from self-loss and being our authentic Self feels like being grounded, rooted in a profound and boundless depth of delicious resonance and alignment. It's a feeling of rightness; a feeling of being *home*. It's the sensation of sitting in front of a fireplace during a cold, snowy day, or jumping into a cold pool on the first scorching-hot day of summer.

Remember Alex from the beginning of the book? The girl who lived a life that did not belong to her? Now that her Self is no longer lost, a day in her life is full of intention. She wakes up and takes a minute to simply check in with herself—with her mind, body, and heart. Her mornings are now her favorite time of day as she throws on a podcast that resonates with her mood, makes coffee, and gets ready. She picks out her clothing—which, by the way, has become more bold lately—and makes a breakfast that feels right for her body in that moment. She got a new job and now shows up to work with a purpose, or at the very least respect for her own efforts. She focuses on her emails when she's writing them and is mentally present for her calls (realizing in the process that work is much more enjoyable when you are truly engaged). Although she still has disagreements, disappointments, and doubts through-out the day, she now notices, validates, and addresses them as they arise. After work, she heads home to read her book-club pick: This month it's *Normal People*—a book she's wanted to read but never felt like she had the time. On Thursdays she heads to a crochet class—she always wanted to know how to do it. She's recently started seeing someone, but hasn't heard from them for a few days. Instead of staring at the phone hop-ing for a text, though, she decides to give them a call. When she goes to bed, she savors the feeling of her pillow pressing against her face. Blowing out a candle, she falls asleep with the satisfaction of knowing she lived that day for, and as, her Self.

Friends, being your Self feels like knowing that you live this day—and every day—on purpose. So observe, feel, and *try* life. Taste it! Everything around you can inform you if you let it. Become vigilant, present, and relentlessly passionate about experiencing the world. Don't let fear limit your decisions. Allow your life to be riddled with lessons and triumphs—moments of intensity and sorrow, as well as sweetness. Keep asking: *What did I learn about my Self today?*

When you wake up in the morning—instead of rolling over to check your texts, social media accounts, or emails—turn your face toward the sun, feel the way your sheets softly cover your skin. Look at the light streaming through the window. Is it raining? Observe the way droplets race down your window-pane. Get out of bed! Even if you're tired—*feel* your exhaustion. Have a meaningful conversation, whether with someone else or with your Self, while you get ready for the day. Take note of your emotions. What are you afraid of today? What is upsetting you? What might calm you? What brings vitality and passion into your life?

Everything will tell you something, if you can put down the distractions long enough to hear it. Are you scared to approach your life? To let it impact you? Are you open to being touched by your feelings and thoughts, by the things and people around you?

Expose your Self to life! Listen, I get it, I know how vulnerable and scary it can be. Trust your Self enough to sense your own resonance, to know what experiences you want to have and—as important—what experiences you *don't* want. Trust yourself to make decisions that serve you. No one else can understand what it means to be you or live *your* life. It's an intimate knowing that only you are privy to.

So, if you want to know who you are, if you're done being lost, open your eyes. Take responsibility for your freedom and make choices. The discomfort and the effort are worth it. Nothing is more valuable than your sense of Self. Nothing more precious, more worthwhile, more *inimitable*.

———

Will you please do one final visualization with me?

Imagine you're alone, wearing your most comfortable sweater, sitting in an old, worn leather armchair in the middle of a room. Your body fits perfectly in the chair, and with a deep breath, you sink into the comfort. Next to you is a coffee table, clean and smooth, holding numerous books with cracked spines and folded pages marking your favorite passages. You hold your full, warm cup of coffee (or tea, or matcha, pick your passion) and take a sip, feeling the richness of the flavor dance on your tongue. A vintage green lamp next to you is shining its soft light—illuminating your surroundings—assisted by the soothing, crackling flames in the fireplace. A cool breeze from the slightly open window grazes your cheek. You feel relaxed yet wide awake, calm yet energized and excited.

Suddenly, you notice a small ember jolt off a piece of firewood and land on your rug. You immediately understand that unless you choose to stand up and extinguish the spark, your whole existence is in danger. The home—and life—you've built will burn to the ground.

Nothing takes precedence.

You get up and extinguish it.

When you pass by the spot the next day, you notice that there is a faint mark on your rug, reminding you of that one time you almost lost everything . . . but didn't. Because you were aware, and deliberate.

Allow your Self to exist—in the here, in the now.

Become.

Be.

Acknowledgments

It's difficult to write acknowledgments when you truly feel speechless. Writing a book has been a lifelong dream of mine, the most honest form of self-expression, and a journey that I was lucky enough to go on with so many wonderful humans.

Ezra, you met me while I was in the depths of my self-loss and loved me anyway. You've been with me even when I didn't know who the "me" was. You were the safe space and support I needed to create the Self that I now have and love. Without you, I am not sure the person who wrote this book would exist.

Dea, you've always seen so much potential and greatness in me that eventually I couldn't help but see it in my Self. You make it easy for me to be who I am. Thank you.

Lauren Hall! Oh, Lauren! This book, quite literally, wouldn't exist without you. You immediately saw my vision and fought tirelessly to preserve it. Thank you for loving this book as much as I do.

Steve Troha and Jan Baumer (and the whole Folio team). I have no idea what I did to deserve such an amazing team! Your generous hearts and killer instincts are the reason I am here. I can't wait to keep creating with you by my side!

Annie Chagnot! Annie! Annie! We did it! This was a *dense* book (ha!), and you poured your soul into it—thank you. You ensured, above all else, that my voice remained true and clear throughout. I am so grateful to have you as my editor. Thank you for embarking on this wild ride with me!

Whitney Frick, Debbie Aroff, Corina Diez, Michelle Jasmine, Maria Braeckel, and Avideh Bashirrad—and everyone else on The Dial Press team. I am beyond honored to be one of your authors now! Thank you for believing in me and for working so hard to bring this book to the world.

Professor Längle, you've inspired me, taught me, and believed in me. Knowing you has been a privilege.

To my family and friends: I am here because of you. Without you and your support, I wouldn't have had the audacity to speak so loudly about the things that matter to me.

To my readers: This was for you and wouldn't be possible without you. Thank you for making my dreams of becoming a writer come true.

Notes

PART I: The Self

13 **"To dare is to lose":** Source unknown. Most commonly attributed to
Søren Kierkegaard.

CHAPTER 1: What Is Self-Loss?

21 **"causes little stir in the world":** Søren Kierkegaard, "C. The Forms of
Sickness (Despair)," in *The Sickness unto Death: A Christian Psycho-
logical Exposition for Edification and Awakening by Anti-Climacus.*
Translated by Alastair Hannay. London: Penguin Books (2004).

27 **Inner Consent:** See Alfried Längle, "Existential Fundamental Motivation." Paper presented at the 18th World Congress of Psychotherapy,
Trondheim, Norway (2002); Alfried Längle, "The Art of Involving
the Person—Fundamental Motivations as the Structure of the Motivational Process," *European Psychotherapy* 4:1 (2003), 47–58; Alfried
Längle, "The Search for Meaning in Life and the Fundamental Existential Motivations," *Psychotherapy in Australia* 10:1 (2003), 22–27.

CHAPTER 2: What Is the Self?

37 **"the self is a relation":** Søren Kierkegaard, "A. That Despair Is the
Sickness unto Death," in *The Sickness unto Death: A Christian Psychological Exposition for Edification and Awakening by Anti-*

Climacus. Translated by Alastair Hannay. London: Penguin Books (2004).

37 **The Self is defined:** Somogy Varga and Charles Guignon, "Authenticity," in *The Stanford Encyclopedia of Philosophy* (Spring 2020 edition). Edward N. Zalta, editor. https://plato.stanford.edu/archives/spr2020/entries/authenticity/.

38 *Runaway Bride:* Garry Marshall, director. 1999.

39 **"the absurdity of freedom":** Jean-Paul Sartre, *Being and Nothingness: An Essay on Phenomenological Ontology.* Translated by Hazel E. Barnes. London and New York: Routledge Classics (2003), p. 503.

39–40 **"to be free is to":** Jean-Paul Sartre, *Being and Nothingness: An Essay on Phenomenological Ontology.* Translated by Hazel E. Barnes. London and New York: Routledge Classics (2003), p. 152.

42 **"bad faith":** Jean-Paul Sartre, *Being and Nothingness: An Essay on Phenomenological Ontology.* Translated by Hazel E. Barnes. London and New York: Routledge Classics (2003), p. 68ff.

42 **To depict this point:** Jean-Paul Sartre, *Being and Nothingness: An Essay on Phenomenological Ontology.* Translated by Hazel E. Barnes. London and New York: Routledge Classics (2003), pp. 82–83.

44 **Kierkegaard suggested:** Søren Kierkegaard, *The Sickness unto Death: A Christian Psychological Exposition for Edification and Awakening by Anti-Climacus.* Translated by Alastair Hannay. London: Penguin Books (2004).

44 **Necessities are certain:** Anoop Gupta, *Kierkegaard's Romantic Legacy: Two Theories of the Self.* Ottawa, Canada: University of Ottawa Press (2005). https://www.jstor.org/stable/j.ctt1ckpgbc.5.

44 **This is why Kierkegaard:** Anoop Gupta, *Kierkegaard's Romantic Legacy: Two Theories of the Self.* Ottawa, Canada: University of Ottawa Press (2005). https://www.jstor.org/stable/j.ctt1ckpgbc.5.

45 **"Everything can be taken from a man":** Viktor E. Frankl, *Man's Search for Meaning.* Boston: Beacon Press (2006), p. 66.

45 **"Freedom is what we do":** Jean-Paul Sartre, *L'Être et le Néant: Essai d'ontologie Phénoménologique.* Paris: Gallimard (1943), p. 528.

46 **"It is not freedom from conditions":** Viktor E. Frankl, *Man's Search for Meaning.* Boston: Beacon Press (2006), p. 130.

46 **Martin Heidegger, a German philosopher:** *Heidegger's Being and Time: Critical Essays.* Richard Polt, editor. Lanham, MD: Rowman & Littlefield (2005).

47 **To be inauthentic:** "Heidegger's Anti Dualism: Beyond Mind and

Body," in *Heidegger's Being and Time: Critical Essays*. Richard Polt, editor. Lanham, MD: Rowman & Littlefield (2005).

48 **They are not alone:** Søren Kierkegaard, "B. The Generality of This Sickness (Despair)," in *The Sickness unto Death: A Christian Psychological Exposition for Edification and Awakening by Anti-Climacus*. Translated by Alastair Hannay. London: Penguin Books (2004).

50 **Here is an example:** Jean-Paul Sartre, *Existentialism Is a Humanism*. Translated by Carol Macomber. New Haven and London: Yale University Press (2007), pp. 30–31.

51 **When translated, this German:** Somogy Varga and Charles Guignon, "Authenticity," in *The Stanford Encyclopedia of Philosophy* (Spring 2020 edition). Edward N. Zalta, editor. https://plato.stanford.edu/archives/spr2020/entries/authenticity/.

51 **"There is no doubt that":** Jean-Paul Sartre, *Being and Nothingness: An Essay on Phenomenological Ontology*. Translated by Hazel E. Barnes. London and New York: Routledge Classics (2003), p. 476.

CHAPTER 3: What Is Life Asking of Me?

62 **"If you have your why":** Friedrich Nietzsche, *Twilight of the Idols: Or, How to Philosophize with the Hammer*. Translated by Richard Polt. Introduction by Tracy Strong. Indianapolis and Cambridge: Hackett (1997), p. 6.

63 **However, meaning is the very thing:** Viktor E. Frankl, *Man's Search for Meaning*. Boston: Beacon Press (2006), p. 99.

63 **Längle considers meaning to:** Alfried Längle, "The Existential Fundamental Motivations Structuring the Motivational Process," *Motivation, Consciousness and Self-Regulation*. D. Leontiev, editor. New York: Nova Science Publishers, Inc. (2012), pp. 27–38.

67 **Frankl compared it to:** Viktor E. Frankl, *Man's Search for Meaning*. Boston: Beacon Press (2006), p. 108.

68 **"What matters, therefore":** Viktor E. Frankl, *Man's Search for Meaning*. Boston: Beacon Press (2006), p. 108.

70 **Frankl proposes that we:** Viktor E. Frankl, *Man's Search for Meaning*. Boston: Beacon Press (2006), p. 111.

70 **"When we are no longer":** Viktor E. Frankl, *Man's Search for Meaning*. Boston: Beacon Press (2006), p. 112.

71 **He was inconsolable:** Viktor E. Frankl, *Man's Search for Meaning*. Boston: Beacon Press (2006), pp. 112–13.

72 **"For the secret of men's being":** Fyodor Dostoyevsky, *The Brothers*

Karamazov. Translated by Constance Garnett. Encyclopedia Britannica, Inc. (1984), p. 131.

72 **"on the meaning of human existence"**: Viktor E. Frankl, *Man's Search for Meaning*. Boston: Beacon Press (2006), pp. 98–99.

72 **"During psychoanalysis"**: Viktor E. Frankl, *Man's Search for Meaning*. Boston: Beacon Press (2006), p. 98.

73 **"I consider it a dangerous"**: Viktor E. Frankl, *Man's Search for Meaning*. Boston: Beacon Press (2006), p. 105.

PART II: The Self You Lost

77 **"The world will ask you"**: Carl G. Jung, "Introduction: Our Schizoid World," in *Love and Will*. New York and London: Norton (1969), p. 15.

CHAPTER 4: What Causes Self-Loss?

90 **"If you do not express"**: Rollo May, "What Is Courage?" in *The Courage to Create*. New York and London: Norton (1994), Kindle edition, p. 15.

91 **"The fear of finding oneself"**: André Gide, *The Immoralist*. Translated by Dorothy Bussy. New York: Vintage Books (1930), p. 89.

97 **"despair is the price"**: Irvin D. Yalom, *When Nietzsche Wept: A Novel of Obsession*. New York: Harper Perennial (2010), Chapter 12.

98 **"The real question is"**: Irvin D. Yalom, *When Nietzsche Wept: A Novel of Obsession*. New York: Harper Perennial (2010), Chapter 8.

102 **Please indulge me**: Nancy Meyers, director. *The Holiday*. 2006.

CHAPTER 5: How Does Society Perpetuate Self-Loss?

111 **Heidegger wrote about**: Martin Heidegger, "The Problem of the Attestation of an Authentic Existentiell Possibility," in *Being and Time*. Translated by Joan Stambaugh. Albany: State University of New York Press (2010).

111 **"This process can be reversed"**: Martin Heidegger, "The Problem of the Attestation of an Authentic Existentiell Possibility," in *Being and Time*. Translated by Joan Stambaugh. Albany: State University of New York Press (2010).

113 **"Every human being must have a point"**: Rollo May, in Connie Robertson's *Wordsworth Dictionary of Quotations* (1998), p. 270. (The quote seems to come from a 1967 *Psychology Today* interview with Mary Harrington Hall.)

115 **"faulty interpretations":** Martin Heidegger, *The Basic Problems of Phenomenology,* rev. ed. Translated by Albert Hofstadter. Blooming-ton and Indianapolis: Indiana University Press (1988), p. 322.

117 **Let's go through these prerequisites:** Alfried Längle, *Existential Therapy: Legacy, Vibrancy, and Dialogue.* L. Barnett and G. Madison, editors. New York: Routledge (2012), pp. 159–70.

127 **"If I let myself really understand":** Carl R. Rogers, *On Becoming a Person: A Therapist's View on Psychotherapy.* Boston: Houghton Mifflin Company (1961), p. 18.

132 **"We must become so alone":** Hermann Hesse, *Reflections.* Translated by Ralph Manheim. London: Triad/Panther Books (1979), p. 57.

134 **But as cliché as it sounds:** Alexander Pope, "Part II," in *An Essay on Criticism.* Originally published in 1711.

CHAPTER 6: Where Do I End and Others Begin?

150 **We set a reflexive boundary:** Alfried Längle, "The Search for Meaning in Life and the Existential Fundamental Motivations," *International Journal of Existential Psychology & Psychotherapy* 1:1 (2004), 28; Alfried Längle, "The Art of Involving the Person—Fundamental Motivations as the Structure of the Motivational Process," *European Psychotherapy* 4:1 (2003), 47–58.

PART III: The Self You Live

163 **"I have been and still am a seeker":** Hermann Hesse, *Demian.* Translated by W. J. Strachan. London: Peter Owen Vision Press (1958), p. 6.

CHAPTER 7: Mental Decluttering: Create Space for Who You Really Are

178 **Even sex began to evoke a sense:** Megan Oaten, Richard J. Stevenson, Mark A. Williams, Anina N. Rich, Marino Butko, and Trevor I. Case, "Moral Violations and the Experience of Disgust and Anger," *Behavioral Neuroscience* 12 (August 22, 2018). https://doi.org/10.3389/fnbeh.2018.00179; J. Haidt, "The Moral Emotions," in *Handbook of Affective Sciences.* R. J. Davidson, K. R. Scherer, & H. H. Goldsmith, editors. Oxford, UK: Oxford University Press (2003), pp. 852–70.

185 **"How should the new day":** Martin Heidegger, *Ponderings VII–XI: Black Notebooks 1938–1939.* Translated by Richard Rojcewicz. Bloomington and Indianapolis: Indiana University Press (2017), p. 49.

185 **"These faulty interpretations":** Martin Heidegger, *The Basic Prob-*

lems of Phenomenology, rev. ed. Translated by Albert Hofstadter. Bloomington and Indianapolis: Indiana University Press (1988), p. 322.

CHAPTER 8: The Body Electric: Reconnect and Communicate with Your Body

192 **"the body is our general":** Maurice Merleau-Ponty, *Phenomenology of Perception.* Translated by Colin Smith. London and New York: Routledge Classics (2002), p. 169.

192 **"Inside and outside are inseparable":** Maurice Merleau-Ponty, *Phenomenology of Perception.* Translated by Colin Smith. London and New York: Routledge Classics (2002), p. 474.

193 **Simply put, our body is:** Maurice Merleau-Ponty, *Phenomenology of Perception.* Translated by Colin Smith. London and New York: Routledge Classics (2002), p. 167.

194 **A famous example Sartre offers:** Jean-Paul Sartre, *Being and Nothingness: An Essay on Phenomenological Ontology.* Translated by Hazel E. Barnes. London and New York: Routledge Classics (2003).

194 *l'être-pour-soi:* Jean-Paul Sartre, *Being and Nothingness: An Essay on Phenomenological Ontology.* Translated by Hazel E. Barnes. London and New York: Routledge Classics (2003), p. 650.

194 *l'être-pour-autrui:* Jean-Paul Sartre, *Being and Nothingness: An Essay on Phenomenological Ontology.* Translated by Hazel E. Barnes. London and New York: Routledge Classics (2003), p. 650.

207 **You've all seen *Mean Girls*, right?:** Mark Waters, director. *Mean Girls,* 2004.

CHAPTER 9: Feel It All: Experience and Express Your Emotions

224 **More specifically, she says:** Jill Bolte Taylor, *My Stroke of Insight: A Brain Scientist's Personal Journey.* New York: Viking (2006), p. 146.

225 **Dr. Jill answers this question:** Jill Bolte Taylor, *My Stroke of Insight: A Brain Scientist's Personal Journey.* New York: Viking (2006), p. 155.

225 **"transition through personal freedom":** Alfried Längle, *Emotionality: An Existential-Analytical Understanding and Practice.* https:// laengle.info/userfile/doc/Emotionality-incompl.pdf, p. 52.

226 **"detect the personally relevant":** Alfried Längle, *Emotionality: An Existential-Analytical Understanding and Practice.* https:// laengle .info/userfile/doc/Emotionality-incompl.pdf, p. 44.

235 **Existentially, tears tell us:** Alfried Längle, *Emotionality: An Existential-*

Analytical Understanding and Practice. https://laengle.info/userfile/ doc/Emotionality-incompl.pdf, p. 59.

PART IV: The Self You Are

245   **"One thing I feel":** Irvin D. Yalom, *When Nietzsche Wept: A Novel of Obsession*. New York: Harper Perennial (2010), Chapter 21.

CHAPTER 10: The Art of Being Your Self

253   **"Nothing determines me":** Maurice Merleau-Ponty, *Phenomenology of Perception*. Translated by Colin Smith. London and New York: Routledge Classics (2002), p. 530.

Recommended Reading

Beauvoir, Simone de. *Memoirs of a Dutiful Daughter.*
Camus, Albert. *The Myth of Sisyphus.*
———. *The Stranger.*
Didion, Joan. *The Year of Magical Thinking.*
Dostoevsky, Fyodor. *Notes from the Underground.*
Ellison, Ralph. *Invisible Man.*
Frankl, Viktor E. *Man's Search for Meaning.*
Heidegger, Martin. *Being and Time.*
Hesse, Hermann. *Demian.*
———. *Siddhartha.*
Kafka, Franz. *The Metamorphosis.*
Kierkegaard, Søren. *Either/Or.*
———. *The Sickness unto Death: A Christian Psychological Exposition for Edification and Awakening by Anti-Climacus.*
Längle, Alfried. *Existenzanalyse und Logotherapie.*

———. *Existenzanalyse.*

———. *Living Your Own Life: Existential Analysis in Action.*

Merleau-Ponty, Maurice. *Phenomenology of Perception.*

Nietzsche, Friedrich. *The Will to Power.*

Sartre, Jean-Paul. *Being and Nothingness: An Essay on Phenomenological Ontology.*

———. *Nausea.*

———. *No Exit.*

Whitman, Walt. "I Sing the Body Electric," in *Leaves of Grass.*

ABOUT THE AUTHOR

DR. SARA KUBURIC is an existential psychotherapist, consultant, writer, and columnist for *USA Today*. She is often known as the Millennial Therapist due to her Instagram handle and large online presence. She was born in Yugoslavia and raised in Canada. She is passionate about helping people seeking change. Her interest in psychology stems from her personal experience living through wars, navigating complex relationships, and continually learning what it means to be human.

sara-kuburic.com
Instagram: @millennial.therapist
sarakuburic.substack.com

ABOUT THE TYPE

This book was set in Sabon, a typeface designed by the well-known German typographer Jan Tschichold (1902–74). Sabon's design is based upon the original letter forms of sixteenth-century French type designer Claude Garamond and was created specifically to be used for three sources: foundry type for hand composition, Linotype, and Monotype. Tschichold named his typeface for the famous Frankfurt typefounder Jacques Sabon (c. 1520–80).

The Dial Press, an imprint of Random House,
publishes books driven by the heart.

Follow us on Instagram:
@THEDIALPRESS

Discover other Dial Press books and
sign up for our e-newsletter:

thedialpress.com